REHABILITATION AND RESETTLEMENT IN TEHRI HYDRO POWER PROJECT

REHABILITATION AND RESETTLEMENT IN TEHRI HYDRO POWER PROJECT

A Amarender Reddy

PARTRIDGE

To order additional copies of this book, contact
Partridge India
000 800 10062 62
orders.india@partridgepublishing.com

www.partridgepublishing.com/india

Contents

Foreword

Ever since independence, India has been undertaking a number of development projects as a part of its planned development strategy. Large irrigation and power projects have been on the top of the agenda of development. While the benefits are not in doubt, these projects have also been the major cause of submergence of large tracts of land, disturbance to ecological balance and displacement of millions of people from their original place of habitation and livelihood. Development induced displacement in the country has brought severe environmental problems as much as social and economic distress to the displaced people. By the 1980s the magnitude of project displaced people reached several millions triggering nation-wide people's movements against large projects, which brought the issue of fair resettlement and rehabilitation to the fore. Until then resettlement and rehabilitation received least priority in project planning either by the Central or the state governments, and the measures remained ad hoc without any systematic planning. With the mobilization of project affected people and the unfolding of the politics of people's movements, governments at the Centre and the state levels were forced to consider resettlement and rehabilitation as a part of project planning. Beginning with 2003 the National Resettlement Rehabilitation Policy (NRRP) went through several refinements resulting in the modified version in 2007, and with further modifications finally as the NRRP 2009.

It was in the context of the growing awareness of the adverse consequences of large dams, that Tehri Hydro Power Project was conceived and executed.

There were widespread protests against it from the environmentalists and the potential people to be displaced. The period of execution of the project spread over almost three decades (1978-2008) was also the period of growing people's resistance to large dams which ensued informed debate and demand for concrete policy for resettlement and rehabilitation. The expectation was that Tehri Hydro Power Project would have imbibed the emerging consensus for fair resettlement and rehabilitation. Though at that time 'social impact assessment' as a precondition for project design and implementation was still in the early stages of Resettlement and Rehabilitation Policy, the Tehri Hydro Power Project authorities sponsored a socio-economic survey of the project affected people (PAPs). In 1993, the Administrative Staff College of India (ASCI), Hyderabad conducted a baseline survey of the prospective project affected people. And this was followed by a second survey by ASCI in 2008, the year of completion of the Tehri project, to assess the socio-economic condition of PAPs who were resettled, and were in the process of being rehabilitated. This monograph is based on the results of the ASCI surveys. The evaluation of the condition of the PAPs are done by adopting Michael M. Cernea's 'risk and reconstruction model', which has already been tested to be appropriate for the analysis of development induced displacement situation in the country.

Resettlement and Rehabilitation, however ideally conceived often end up in extensive discontentment and deprivation among the displaced people. Capacity for undertaking sustainable resettlement is constrained by conservative thinking on the nature of rehabilitation purely in terms of ex-ante compensation. The result is an upfront under budgeting R & R with the objective of pushing the costs to lowest levels in hoping to meet the economic viability proposals of the development projects. Tehri Dam experience seems to be a departure from this experience.

The study shows that the overall socio-economic conditions of the affected people have been better than the place of origin. Access to schooling, school infrastructure and the education levels improved in the resettled New Tehri Town as wells as in the new villages. Access to land of those who opted 'land for land' increased both in terms of average size and in irrigation facilities. Instances of growing three crops including high value vegetable crops by marginal farmers with an average of half an acre of land was observed. And land values in the resettled villages were much higher than at the origin. Overall housing conditions improved, and landless households were provided free one-room pucca houses. New employment opportunities were available especially for those migrating to the urban settlement. There was smooth social assimilation of displaced persons in their new villages where they were resettled. Overall consumption levels and access to food, and access to health facilities, and quality and connectivity of roads were better except in a few villages which are cut-off by the new reservoir. Extension and marketing facilities appear to be lagging in enabling the farmers to get the best out of the improved access to land and irrigation. There may be still much more potential that is yet to be realized, but overall the story of rehabilitation of PAPs of Tehri Dam is a refreshingly encouraging contrast compared to the past distressing experience of R & R of most of the development projects.

The unwritten story of the book is that the difference Tehri R & R makes owes much to the mobilization of people of Tehri region as much as the parallel people's movements that were witnessed at that time across the country for fair deal to the project affected people. The book vividly brings out the Tehri model which could as well be an example that could further be improved to arrive at an acceptable method of implementation of an ideal resettlement and rehabilitation policy in the country.

D. Narasimha Reddy
Visiting Professor
Institute for Human Development
New Delhi

Chapter 1

Introduction

Compulsory land acquisition and involuntary displacement for construction of mega development projects is a major challenge for rehabilitation and resettlement of project effected people (like construction of Three-Gorges Dam in China to generate about 22,250 megawatts of power resulted in 1.24 million people to lose their homes under the rising water). Construction of mega projects is mostly to generate hydro-power, irrigation and flood control which benefit millions of the people but also displaces many people. In fact it is well established now that underestimation of number of project effected people is the norm rather than the exception (China Report 1999, Scudder 1997, McCully 1996). Rehabilitation and resettlement of project effected people (people displaced from their original habitation due to construction of mega projects) across the world is a major task of governments across the world. The first prime minister of India, Jawahar Lal Nehru gave more emphasis on construction of mega irrigation and power projects, by calling them as Temples of modern India. Along with the construction of mega projects, Government of India also gave equal importance in rehabilitation and resettlement of project effected people. There are a number of mega multipurpose hydro-power projects in India. The Koyna hydroelectric dam, Srisailam dam, Nathpa jhakri dam, Sardar sarovar dam, Bhakra-nangal dam, Indirasagar dam, Nagarjuna Sagar dam, Idukki dam, Hirakud dam and Tehri hydro project. In India about 50 million project effected people have been rehabilitated since independence (Somayaji and Talwar 2011). Tehri hydro project was one of the largest multipurpose project on Bhagirathi river in north India. This book explores the impact of rehabilitation and resettlement package on the project effected people of this mega project. In this book, socio-economic development of project effected people in the context of the real freedoms that the citizens enjoy, to pursue the objectives they have reason to value, and in this sense the expansion of human capability" (Dreze and Sen 1996:10). This book explores the experience of project effected people in adjusting to the new environment in resettled areas? What steps have been taken by the implementing agencies for the benefit of the project effected people? What can be done to improve the socio-economic stand of the resettled people with in-depth field studies in the tehri hydro-project effected areas. Tehri dam site was identified as a potential site for a storage dam in 1949. A reconnaissance survey of Bhagirathi river valley was carried out during 1961–62 to select a suitable site for constructing a storage dam, wherein Tehri site was found techno-economically feasible for the construction of a high earth- and rock-fill dam. The Planning Commission approved the project in 1972. THDC was set up in 1988 as a joint venture of GoI and GoUP for the implementation of the Tehri hydropower complex (2,400 mW), with equity participation by GoI and GoUP in the ratio of 3:1 for power component, while the irrigation component (20% of Tehri dam and HPP cost) was to be entirely funded by the GoUP. GoUP transferred project works to THDC in 1989.

Tehri dam is one of the highest earth- and rock-fill dams in the world. A 260.5 m high earth- and rock-fill dam was constructed on the Ganga River at the downstream of the confluence of its two main tributaries—i.e. Bhagirathi and Bhilangana rivers. At crest, the length of the dam is 570 m and the width is 25.5 m, flared to 30.5 m at abutments. The THDC and government of Uttaranchal are following the best practices in its rehabilitation and resettlement of the oustees. An expert committee headed by Prof. Hanumantha Rao on the environmental and rehabilitation aspects of Tehri dam was constituted by the government in 1996, and the committee submitted its report in 1997. Construction of the powerhouse and main dam started in 1996 and 1997 respectively.

Tehri hydropower project (THPP) (1,000 mW) was completed in 2006–07, and the benefits of the project with respect to irrigation, drinking water, and electricity already started to flow with the commissioning of the generating units. Presently, THDC has seven projects under various stages of investigations in

Ganga valley while two projects are under active construction. The catchment area of the river at Tehri dam site is 7,511 sq. km, and the dam shall impound the monsoon flows of the river to create a lake with surface spread of 44 sq. km.

Major benefits of the Tehri project are:

1. Generate clean and renewable energy of 2,400 mW during peak hours with lower cost of operation and maintenance.
2. Provide an additional irrigation facility to 2.7 lakh ha of land and stabilization of existing irrigated land of 6.04 lakh ha.
3. Provide 500 cusecs of drinking water to Delhi and UP.
4. Moderate the flood during monsoon by way of storage of excess water.
5. Develop pisciculture.
6. Integrate the development of the catchment area, including afforestation and soil conservation of 36,200 ha. of severely eroded land.
7. Develop tourism in the Garhwal region, which shall boost the employment opportunities.

The completion of Tehri dam project was a landmark achievement in the history of river valley projects in the country. This project is a unique multi-purpose project which provides benefits of electricity, irrigation, and drinking water to the northern India. The benefits from the project have already started to flow. The Tehri hydropower station is now operational with three units of 250 mW, each having been commissioned. The project, with its technical complexities, is an engineering marvel. The rehabilitation and resettlement works carried out in Tehri project have been on a massive scale.

About the book

This book is aimed at exploring the socio-economic assessment of the project effected people of Tehri-hydro project. The Administrative Staff College of India (ASCI), Hyderabad first conducted a socio-economic study for the THDC in 1993, which aimed at the families to be rehabilitated and those already rehabilitated. The first socio-economic study carried out a benchmark survey to evaluate the project and its impact and to build a socio-economic profile of the households to understand the conditions before and after the R

& R. The survey also documented the perceptions, views, and suggestions of the rehabilitated households.

The present book is a follow up to the previous study, and it compares with the results of the first survey to understand any changes. The main aim of the book is to understand the socio-economic conditions of the households rehabilitated and resettled up to the year 2008.

Scope of the Book

To understand the current status of the project-affected population (PAP), a household survey has been conducted in the year 2007. There are different varieties of PAPs (agriculturists, artisans, businessmen, people who have opted for cash-only compensation, etc.). The study tried to contact these people and find out their socio-economic conditions after rehabilitation. In general, the impact of the R & R package was analysed with respect to the change in the R & R initiatives over two different periods, viz. 1993 and 2007. The study covered all the households which were categorized into (1) agriculture and related activities taken up by those receiving 'land for land' compensation, (2) income-generation activities that have sustained over the period, (3) new tertiary (service) activities that have gained ground, (4) PAFs who have opted for cash compensation, (5) partially affected people who have upgraded their skills, (6) people living in the cut-off areas and who now have new modes of connectivity, and (7) other issues of social development measures among the PAFs.

Basic Theoretical Framework of the Methodology

Impoverishment risks and reconstruction (IRR) model was adopted in the study. The field survey has been designed based on the IRR model, which assesses the intrinsic risks that cause impoverishment through displacement, as well as the effectiveness of the rehabilitation policy to counteract—eliminate or mitigate—these risks through rehabilitation and resettlement. The model basically explains what happens during massive displacements and risk assessment. It also assesses the safeguarding measures to mitigate the risks due to displacement during rehabilitation and resettlement. We believe that this impoverishment risks and reconstruction (IRR) model substantively adds to the tools of explaining, diagnosing, assessing, predicting, and planning the effectiveness of R & R policy implementation.

The components of the model are:

a. landlessness
b. joblessness
c. homelessness
d. marginalization
e. food insecurity
f. increased morbidity
g. loss of access to common property resources
h. community disarticulation.

The model studies the methods employed in rehabilitation and resettlement in preventing or overcoming the pattern of impoverishment, risk reversal, or mitigation. The model basically studies the reconstruction strategies implemented and the operational performance based on the following parameters:

a. from landlessness to land-based resettlement
b. from joblessness to reemployment
c. from homelessness to house reconstruction
d. from marginalization to social inclusion
e. from increased morbidity to improved healthcare
f. from food insecurity to adequate nutrition
g. from loss of access to restoration of community assets and services
h. from social disarticulation to networks and community rebuilding.

The model stimulates the generation of hypotheses about relations between key variables in both displacement and relocation. The research utility of the model comes from its ability to guide data collection in the field and coherently aggregate disparate empirical findings along the model's key variables. Hence, IRR model chosen as a guiding framework for conducting and organizing fieldwork. Overall, the adoption of this model provides the basis for assessing the effectiveness of the reestablishment of resettlers along several clear indicators.

a. how impoverishment risks have been successfully attacked and reversed
b. the livelihood reconstruction strategies devolved over a period of time and the specific directions identified.

Usefulness of IRR Model in the Current Context

Evidence indicates that the IRR framework is in some important respects ahead of the current mainstream practices. It builds upon the more advanced scholarly analyses of implementation of resettlement package. The model is fully compatible with the most advanced resettlement policies in existence today and offers a methodology capable to vastly increase consistency and effectiveness in the implementation of these policies.

Sampling

There were 125 villages and 1 Tehri town affected by the construction of the Tehri project. Out of these, 37 villages were fully submerged, and 88 villages were partially submerged.

The rehabilitation work was divided into two parts: (*a*) urban rehabilitation and (*b*) rural rehabilitation. Old Tehri Town and 125 villages were affected as a result of implementation of the Tehri dam project. New Tehri Town has been established in place of Old Tehri town through the project in which the displaced families of Old Tehri Town were rehabilitated. The rural rehabilitation sites are: (*a*) Dehradun district, (*b*) Haridwar district, and (*c*) New Tehri.

Under urban rehabilitation, all the 5,291 families of Old Tehri Town (categorized as fully affected) were completely rehabilitated, and the Old Tehri Town was vacated in January 2004. Under rural rehabilitation, 5,429 fully affected families have been rehabilitated through the allotment of land or cash compensation. In partially affected villages, out of 2,074 fully affected rural families, 1,572 families have been rehabilitated while R & R of the balance rural families is underway.

The sample of the households was drawn using two-stage sampling procedure. In the first stage, the villages were selected based on probability proportion in consultation with the officials of the THDC engaged in the rehabilitation of affected families. At the second stage, 350 households were selected based on the random sample. Out of 350 sample households, 200 were rural households, and 150 were urban households. The urban families were selected from New Tehri Town since it is the only affected urban settlement in the project area. The rural families were selected from ten different rehabilitated colonies in probability proportion to PAFs in the rehabilitated site.

The data for the rural rehabilitation were collected from 42 households in Pashulok, 31 in Banjarawala, 25 in Baniawala, 16 in Dehrakhas, 10 in Raiwala, and 5 in Atakfarm in the Dehradun district, 15 in Pathri block 1, 20 in Pathri block 2, 28 in Pathri block 3, and 8 in Pathri Rao/Suman nagar in the Haridwar district. The data for the urban rehabilitation were collected from 150 households in New Tehri Town, which includes Mooldhar and Baurari. In addition to the above PAFs, data were collected from a sample of 20 institutions, including schools, banks, temples, and government offices.

Explaining the Questionnaire

For the purpose of the study, questionnaires for both urban and rural surveys were developed in English and then translated into Hindi on the advice of THDC and the officials of the Rehabilitation Directorate, Uttaranchal. This was done since Hindi is the local language in the surveyed area. The questionnaire was thoroughly discussed with the THDC officials before conducting the survey and incorporated the necessary modifications as advised. The household survey was conducted in both the rural and urban rehabilitated colonies using structured questionnaires (separate for both rural and urban PAPs).

Detailed data were collected from the affected households on various aspects, such as the size of the family, age, sex, education, main occupation, and number of days of employment in a year of all the family members both before and after rehabilitation. For this purpose, 2007 was taken as the study period. Wherever possible, the data were collected both before rehabilitation and after rehabilitation. This can give an overall idea about how the socio-economic structure of the family has changed because of their displacement. The detailed information regarding assets possessed, such as house, land, cattle, agricultural implements, household items, and vehicles, was culled out both before and after displacement to estimate how the lifestyle has changed. Detailed information regarding the income from various sources, like agriculture and allied activities, cottage industries, non-agricultural income, labour (both skilled and unskilled), government service, and the other occupation and expenditure incurred on food, education, cloths, health, fuel for vehicle, entertainment and others was collected. This gives a broad picture about how the PAPs are affected economically because of the displacement. They have received from the THDC the information about the various types of compensation/allowances (such as incentive allowances, compensation allowances, building construction assistance allowances, decoration allowances, replacement allowances, food and seed allowances) and the property they have lost, such as land (irrigated or unirrigated), trees, buildings, shops, etc.

Data on the distance and the satisfactory levels on the civic facilities (such as hospital, education, water for drinking and irrigation, roads, sanitation, electricity, financial institutions, markets/shops, communication, entertainment, religious places, parks, function halls, fuel, pastured land, village pond, graveyard, etc.) created/provided by the THDC in those rehabilitated colonies were also collected and compared with the amenities they had earlier in their villages. From this, the estimated how these facilities were utilized by the community as an individual or in-group.

The data on the perspective of the project, the rehabilitation site, the transfer of property, etc., as well as the status of women at home and in the village, violence on women, freedom in the new place, etc. were also collected.

Household Survey

The study team has visited 11 rehabilitated colonies in three districts (i.e. Dehradun, Haridwar, and Tehri) and collected data from 350 PAPs. Detailed data were collected from 150 urban PAPs, 200 rural PAPs, and 20 institutions during September 2007. The sample villages were Pashulok, Banjarawala, Baniawala, Dehrakhas, Raiwala, Atakfarm, Pathri block 1, Pathri block 2, Pathri block 3, Pathri Rao/Suman nagar, and New Tehri Town. Two separate questionnaires were prepared for both urban and rural respondents in local Hindi language. The data collection team consisting of ten local graduates who were recruited and trained extensively to ensure a standardized approach to data collection. The principal author of this book monitored and supervised the field-level data collection throughout the survey, with necessary logistic assistance of THDC/Rehabilitation Directorate officials.

Detailed data were collected on the family structure and composition and socio-economic conditions of the PAPs, like land structure, cattle information, income, expenditure, cropping pattern, occupational structure, property lost because of the displacement, compensation and other benefits received from the THDC, their concern about the project, construction, usage and satisfactory levels of various community-based infrastructure provided/constructed by the THDC, and the status of the women before and after displacement. The final questionnaires administered to collect data for both urban and rural households are presented in annexures 1 and 2 at the end of chapter 1.

Chapterization

The study presents the introduction and methodology in the first chapter. An overview of the Tehri hydropower project is presented in the second chapter. The rehabilitation and resettlement policy of Tehri dam is presented in the third chapter. The social conditions of urban and rural households were presented in the fourth chapter. Economic conditions of urban and rural households were presented in the fifth chapter. The community aspects of rehabilitation were presented in the sixth chapter. Finally, the conclusions and recommendations were presented in the seventh chapter.

Chapter 2

Tehri Hydropower Project: An Overview

2.1 The Project

There is a tremendous untapped potential for harnessing water from the various Himalayan tributaries and rivers. With origins of these tributaries and rivers in the snow-clad Himalayas, the flow in them is perennial. Tehri dam is the first major attempt to harness this potential, which apart from meeting irrigation requirements also supports power generation.

The project was first conceived in 1949 by Geological Survey of India (GSI) when a team of officers visited the site and prepared a project report. However, the report was kept in cold storage for over ten years. Renewed attention was bestowed in 1961–62 with a reconnaissance survey of Bhagirathi valley to select a suitable site for locating a storage dam. The preliminary investigations examined four alternative sites in the area and found only Tehri to be technically feasible site for the construction of a high rock-fill dam. Detailed surface and subsurface explorations were carried out in 1963 at the Tehri site.

In May 1965, Dr (late) K. L. Rao, the then union minister for irrigation and power, visited the site, and at his suggestions, a number of alternatives for the project were studied. A Russian expert Mr N. N. Yakovlev, along with a member of the Central Water and Power Commission, government of India

(GoI), visited the site in February 1967, and technical details of the project were reviewed. Subsequently, several well-known dam experts, like Cratchlev, Muller, and Cooke, also visited the site and discussed technical details. These discussions led to the conclusion that a rock-fill dam with central clay core and underground power was the best option for this site.

The Irrigation Department (GoUP) submitted a detailed project report to GoI in 1969. The project then envisaged a rock-fill dam 253.50 m high and an underground powerhouse of 600 mW capacity. The project was technically cleared by the Central Water and River Commission and finally approved by the Planning Commission in 1972. While administrative approval of the GoUP was accorded in 1976, advance action on the project was authorized in 1971. However, till 1977–78, the progress on the work was very slow due to paucity of funds, though the various scientific surveys were carried out. The main works were taken up for construction in 1978–79 with funds availability from the state government budget.

From the first initiation in 1969 to the actual progress of work in 1977–78, the power demand in Uttar Pradesh has considerably increased particularly for meeting the peak power requirements. This resulted in the preparation of revised project report with four components identified as below:

1. *Tehri stage 1*: a 260 m high earth- and gravel-fill dam, creating a lake of 42 sq. km behind the dam and an underground powerhouse of 1,000 mW (4 × 250 mW units) capacity.
2. *Tehri stage 2*: having a pumped storage plant of 1,000 mW (2 × 250 mW units) capacity.
3. *Koteshwar dam*: a 103.5 m high concrete dam, 22 km downstream of Tehri dam, with a powerhouse of 400 mW (4 × 100 mW units) capacity.
4. *Associated transmission system*: two circuits of 765 KVA for evacuation of 2,400 mW of power from Tehri to Meerut.

Due to the increase in costs of inputs, the project cost was revised in 1984 and again 1987. The project was originally executed by the Irrigation Department of the GoUP. In 1986, it was decided to convert it into a joint venture project of GoI and the GoUP. Accordingly, the THDC was set up in 1988 to execute the project. In June 1989, THDC was made the sole agency to implement the project, and in the following year, the rehabilitation and resettlement work was also transferred to THDC. An agreement for the financial assistance of Rs. 2,000 crores for the project was reached in November 1986 with the erstwhile USSR. While the Ministry of Environment and Forest accorded forest clearance in June 1987, the environmental clearance was received in July 1989.

Benefits

This project is expected to generate about 6,331 million units of electricity on average availability. The project is designed to provide peak load energy of 2,400 mW. On completion, the project will enhance the electricity generation of existing powerhouses due to availability of renewable water supply throughout the year. The Rishikesh hydel project could generate 900 million units of electricity but currently generating 700 million units. The project is also expected to irrigate 2.7 lakh ha of additional area in the commands of Upper Ganga, Lower Ganga, and Agra canals, besides intensification of the irrigation in another 6 lakh ha. of already irrigated area. On full completion of the project, foodgrain output in the command areas is estimated to increase by 4.27 lakh tonnes, sugar cane by 28.90 lakh tonnes, and fodder by 6 lakh tonnes.

The other benefits expected from the project are moderation of floods, supply of drinking water to the city of Delhi (162 million gallons per day), opportunities to develop pisciculture, promotion of tourism, and generation of employment.

The economic viability of the project was worked out, assuming a 100-years project life, even though as per sediment distribution studies silted-bed level would be reached in 160 years. The cost–benefit ratio for the irrigation part of the project is estimated at 1:2.7.

Project Cost

The total cost of the project, including the investment on transmission system, based on December 1992 prices, comes to Rs. 5,583 crores. The cost of stage 1 works comes to Rs. 2,815 crores, distributed in the ratio of 80:20 between power and irrigation. The cost of stage 2 works is estimated at Rs.

1,224 crores in December 1992 prices. This powerhouse is intended to be used for peaking energy in the existing grid system. The cost of Koteshwar dam project in December 1992 prices is Rs. 725 crores. The 800 KV associated transmission system is estimated to cost Rs. 819 crores in March 1992 prices.

Salient Features: Tehri Dam

Tehri hydropower project (stage 1)

1. Dam

Type	-	earth- and rock-fill dam
Top level	-	839.5 m
Height	-	260.5 m above deepest foundation level
Width at riverbed	-	1,125 m
Width at top	-	20 m flared to 25 m at abutments
Length at top	-	575 m

2. Diversion Tunnels (Horseshoe Type)

On left bank	-	2 nos., 11 m dia., 1,774 and 1,778 m long
On right bank	-	2 nos., 11 m dia., 1,298 and 1,429 m long
Diversion flood discharge	-	8,120 cumecs

3. Reservoir

Catchment area	-	7,511 sq. km
MRL	-	835 m
NRL	-	830 m
Dead storage level	-	740 m
Gross storage	-	3,540 million m^3
Live storage	-	2,615 million m^3

4. Spillways

A. Chute spillways - gated

    i. Crest elevation - 815 m

    ii. Waterway - three bays at 10 m width
two piers, 4 m wide in between

    iii. Design discharge - 5,380 cumecs

    iv. Type and no. of gates - tainter, three

B. Right bank shaft spillways - ungated, two

    i. Crest level - 830.2 m

    ii. Dia. of shaft - 12 m

    iii. Design discharge - 1,900 cumecs each

C. Left bank shaft spillways - gated, two

    i. Crest elevation - 815 m

    ii. Dia. of shaft - 12 m

    iii. Design discharge - 2,200 cumecs each

    iv. Type and no. of gates - tainter, one for each shaft

5. Intermediate Level Outlet

    i. No. and size - one, 8.5 m dia. tunnel

    ii. Discharge capacity at EL 830 m - 1,200 cumecs

6. Powerhouse

    i. Type and no. - underground, two

    ii. Cavity size - $134 \times 22 \times 50$ m (stage 1)
$144 \times 22 \times 65$ m (stage 2)

    iii. Design head - 188 m

    iv. Head race tunnels - four, 8.5 m dia.
total length: 4,441 m

v. Installed capacity   -   1,000 mW (4 × 250 mW) (stage 1)
                               1,000 mW (4 × 250 mW) (stage 2)

7. Cost of Stage 1

i. Total cost excluding   -   Rs. 2,81,500 lakh
    irrigation distribution
    system

ii. Share of irrigation   -   Rs. 56,300 lakh

iii. Share of power   -   Rs. 2,25,200 lakh

iv. Cost of irrigation   -   Rs. 15,516 lakh
    distribution system
    (approx.)

8. Benefits for Stage 1

i. Annual energy at   -   3,532 million units
    busbar (average year)

ii. Additional annual   -   2.70 lakh ha.
    irrigation

iii. Cost of generation   -   Rs. 0.78/unit

iv. Benefit–cost ratio   -   2.7
    (approx.)

9. Tehri Pump Storage Plant (Stage 2)

i. Total cost of the   -   Rs. 1,22,400 lakh
    project

ii. Annual energy   -   1,447 million units
    generation at busbar
    (average year)

iii. Sale rate of energy   -   Rs. 1.77/unit

Salient Features: Koteshwar Dam

1. Dam

Type	-	straight concrete gravity dam
Top level	-	618.5 m
Height above foundation	-	103.5 m

2. Diversion Tunnel

Length of tunnel	-	600.0 m
Dia. of tunnel	-	8.0 m
Design discharge	-	670 cumecs

3. Reservoir

MRL	-	615.0 m
NRL	-	612.5 m
Min. draw-down level	-	598.5 m
Gross storage capacity	-	86 million m^3
Live storage capacity	-	36 million m^3

4. Spillway

Type	-	side channel chute spillway
Width	-	84 m
Crest elevation	-	597.0 m
Design discharge	-	12,000 cumecs
No. and size of bays	-	four, 18 m wide
Energy dissipation device	-	flip bucket

5. Powerhouse

Type	-	surface
Head		
a. Maximum	-	81.0 m
b. Minimum	-	64.5 m

Installed capacity   -   400 mW

Firm power   -   141 mW

6. Cost

Total cost of project   -   Rs. 72,500 lakh

7. Benefits

i.   Annual Energy at busbar   -   1,352 million units
     (average year)

ii. Cost of generation   -   Rs. 0.64/unit

Chapter 3

Rehabilitation and Resettlement Policy of Tehri Dam Project: Meeting the Needs and Aspirations of the People

Construction of large storage dams involves large-scale submergence of land, often resulting in displacement of people. Implementation of rehabilitation and resettlement involves acquisition of land in submergence area as well as in resettlement colonies besides creation of other civic, public, and infrastructural facilities. Acquisition of land for public purpose displaces people, forcing them to give up their homes, assets, and means of livelihood. Apart from depriving them of their lands, livelihood, and resource base, displacement has other traumatic psychological and sociocultural consequences.

Due to the construction of the project, around 5,200 ha. area was submerged. Old Tehri Town and 35 villages were fully submerged, and 74 villages were partially submerged. Under urban rehabilitation, 5,291 families living in Old Tehri Town were treated as fully affected. Under rural rehabilitation, 5,429 are fully affected families, and 3,810 are partially affected families, which are not to be relocated.

The THDC prepared the R & R policy, keeping in mind the various basic principles, needs, and aspirations of the affected people and international best practices. R & R policy of Tehri dam project was prepared with the aim to improve the overall economic status of the project-affected families (PAFs) by providing opportunities in the fields of sustainable income, health, education, sanitation, water supply, communication, and such other areas.

3.1 Basic Principles and Objectives Guiding the Formulation of R & R Policy

1. To minimize the displacement and to identify non-displacing or least-displacing alternatives.
2. To plan for the R & R of project-affected families (PAFs), including special needs of women, tribals, SC/ST, and other vulnerable sections.
3. To provide better standard of living to PAFs.
4. To compensate rural oustees through allotment of agricultural land or cash in lieu thereof. Land-for-land option is preferred.
5. To settle the rural oustees in large blocks so that the fabric of their social life remains intact.
6. To involve oustees or their representatives to the extent possible in selected rehabilitation centres and other issues to facilitate harmonious relationship between the project proponent and the PAFs.
7. To provide community facilities at rural rehabilitation centres even if these did not exist at their earlier settlements.
8. To assess the requirement of other public facilities, connectivity, and infrastructure requirements of affected population who will continue to reside above submergence level.
9. To study employment needs and self-employment-generation schemes.

3.2 Rehabilitation Provisions

Background

Due to the construction of the Tehri Complex, a total area of 5,200 ha. has been submerged. With this, the Old Tehri Town and 37 villages (including 2 of Koteshwar) were under full submergence, while another 88 villages (including 14 of Koteshwar) were only partially affected. In addition, 13 more villages were affected for the construction of infrastructural facilities, like workshop, project colony, and the New Tehri Town developed for rehabilitating the urban population.

Rehabilitation Plan

The rehabilitation plan has been broadly divided into rural rehabilitation and urban rehabilitation. Affected families under rural rehabilitation were categorized as fully affected or partially affected. The families whose 50% or more land was acquired were treated as fully affected. Those families with less than 50% land coming under submergence were categorized as partially affected.

Old tehri tower sub-merged in to water

In case of urban population of Tehri town, all 5,291 families living in the town as on the cut-off date of 6 June 1985 were treated as fully affected. Under rural rehabilitation, 5,429 fully affected families due to Tehri dam were to be rehabilitated. Another 3,810 rural families were partially affected and were not displaced; they were paid cash compensation for their land under submergence or allotted equal land above submergence level. The urban rehabilitation programme involved a total of 5,291 families, covered within the cut-off date of June 1985.

Full submergence of old tehri town

Water reservoir after construction of dam

Implementation

As per government decision, R & R works were transferred to the UP state government in January 1999 for implementation under the control and supervision of the commissioner (Garhwal) with funds to be provided by THDC. With the formation of Uttaranchal state, R & R has been implemented by the Uttaranchal state government since January 2001.

Broad Features of Rehabilitation Policy

These are the basic principles that guided the formation of the rehabilitation policy:

- Rural oustees should be compensated through the allotment of agricultural land or cash in lieu thereof.
- The rural oustees should be settled in large blocks so that the fabric of their social life remains intact.
- Oustees or their representatives should be involved to the extent possible in selecting the rehabilitation centres.
- To the extent possible, consideration is given to the preference of the oustees for settlement at a particular site.
- Community facilities are provided at each of the rural rehabilitation centres at the cost of the project even if these did not exist at their earlier settlements.

Rehabilitation Package

Within the framework of the set principles which guided the formation of rehabilitation policy, an attractive and a liberal rehabilitation package evolved, which was improved from time to time, including measures approved by the government based on the recommendations of the Hanumantha Rao Committee.

dam construction underway

Water reservoir after dam construction

3.3 The Rehabilitation Package offered to the Project Effected People

Definition of Family

For the purpose of entitlement of rehabilitation benefits to landowners, family is represented by the head of the family, in whose name the land is entered in revenue records as on date of section 4(1) notification, and includes all members dependent on him. In case of death of the landowner (head of family) that took place prior to the issue of section 4(1) notification, all legal heirs become eligible to receive rehabilitation benefits. All major sons and unmarried daughters of entitled fully affected family who has attained the age of 21 years and dependent parent (mother/father) are eligible for ex-gratia payment.

Rural Package
Landowner Family

- Two acres of developed irrigated land or half acre of developed irrigated land adjacent to municipal limits of Dehradun, Haridwar, or Rishikesh cities, or cash of Rs. 5 lakh in lieu of allotment of land as per their option.
- Compensation for acquired land as per Land Acquisition Act plus solatium at 30%. Even if acquired land is less than 2 acres, 2 acres of developed irrigated land is given, cost of which to be adjusted from the amount of compensation payable in respect of acquired land. If the cost of land acquired were more than the cost of the allotted land, the oustees would be paid the difference of cost, and if it is less, the difference in cost will not be recovered.
- The cost of house property/trees acquired to be evaluated at the PWD/forest/horticulture department rates, plus solatium. Further, ex-gratia equivalent to amount of depreciation, subject to a maximum of Rs. 50,000 is payable. Minimum compensation in case of house is Rs. 1.00 lakh.
- Allotment of residential plot of 200 sq. m to each family at nominal cost.

- Cash grant for shifting is Rs. 5,200/- and for seeds/fertilizers is Rs. 4,960/-.
- Additional incentive grant of Rs. 15,000/- payable to those who shift within six months from date of award of compensation or date of allotment of land, whichever is less, after handing over their acquired property.
- All the eligible additional family members for fully affected rural families attaining the age of 21 years as on 19 July 1990, and dependent parent (mother/father) would receive ex-gratia amount equivalent to 750 days of minimum agricultural wage per member.
- Cash grant ranging from Rs. 80,000/- to Rs. 120,000/- to each rural shop holder, depending upon the locations.

Landless Agricultural Labourers

- Land free of cost at 2 acre/½ acre/Rs. 5 lakh cash option, as applicable to rural project affected families on certification by the concerned district magistrate.
- Ex-gratia grant to additional family members as applicable for fully affected rural families.

Urban Package

- Landowners, including Nazul landholders, are given residential plot of various sizes (60, 100, 150, 200, 250, and 300 sq. m) in proportion to their holdings at very nominal cost (ranging from Rs. 5 per sq. m. for plot up to 150 sq. m to Rs. 150 per sq. m for plots of size 300 sq. m) at locations as per choice, in addition to compensation of house property as calculated in case of rural properties (average rate of developed plot is in the range of Rs. 1,000/- per sq. m).
- House construction assistance, as grant to the landowners at the following rates less the compensation already paid:
  - 60–100 sq. m plot holders: Rs. 2.50 lakh
  - 150–200 sq. m plot holders: Rs. 3.50 lakh
  - 250–300 sq. m plot holders: Rs. 4.50 lakh

- Ready-to-build houses/flats to entitled tenant on subsidized cost at pre-1989 rates.
- Benap house owners who constructed house before 6 June 1985 are allotted either house/flats or plots (if available).
- Allotment of shop at subsidized cost (Rs. 1600/- per sq. m) in NTT/Dehradun/Rishikesh to those running shops at Old Tehri Town.
- Compensation for 'Saj-Sajja' for shopkeepers.
- One shop to be allotted to shop owners who were not running shop(s) themselves in Old Tehri Town.
- Cash grant of Rs. 3,000/- to Rs. 4,000/- for transportation of household goods and Rs. 1,500/- to Rs. 2,000/- for commercial goods. In addition, entitled families who hand over their acquired properties and shift to new allotted sites within a period of six months from the date of allotment of plot/flat, an incentive grant of Rs. 12000/- per family is payable.
- One-room flat to economically weaker section (EWS) free of cost, up to a maximum of 100 families.
- All additional eligible family members of entitled landowner families, as per criteria defined under rural package, get ex-gratia amount equivalent to 750 days of minimum agricultural wage per member.
- Cash option allowed in lieu of allotment of plots (Rs. 1.10 lakh to Rs. 3.00 lakh), flat (1.00 lakh), and shop (Rs. 0.25 lakh to Rs. 0.60 lakh).
- The government of Uttaranchal paid cash grant to shopkeepers of Old Tehri Town, ranging from Rs. 1.00 lakh to Rs. 3.00 lakh, depending upon the category of shop.
- The government of Uttaranchal paid cash grant of Rs. 1.50 lakh each to advocates of Old Tehri Town who were practising before the year 1985.

Provision of Social Amenities

The rural resettlement colonies are located in agricultural areas in Dehradun and Haridwar districts and have been provided with all civic facilities, like electricity, irrigation, piped drinking water, roads, schools, dispensaries, places of worship, and community centres. There are around 14 rural resettlement colonies located in agricultural areas (6 in Dehradun district and 8 in Haridwar district) and provided with all basic facilities.

The urban families are resettled at New Tehri Town (NTT) or at Rishikesh and Dehradun as per their option. NTT has all the modern facilities for education, hospital, financial institutions, district administration offices, markets, a bus stand, and places of worship, etc.

It can be seen that the land allotted at resettlement site is approximately four times the land acquired.

The total cost of rehabilitation and resettlement of Tehri dam is around Rs. 1,260 crores, which is around 15% of the cost of the project.

3.4 Evolution of R & R Package

The government of UP commenced the rehabilitation work of the affected families when the project was under them. The rehabilitation policy, including the location of New Tehri Town (NTT), had been evolved and decided by the state government of UP after interaction with the representatives of the local population. After the incorporation of THDC, the rehabilitation work was handed over to the THDC in 1990. The policies evolved by the state government were fully adopted by the corporation, and later on, the amount of compensation was enhanced wherever necessary.

Improvements by Hanumantha Rao Committee (HRC) in 1998

On the demands for further improvements raised by the local population, the government of India in September 1996 constituted a committee, viz. Hanumantha Rao Committee (HRC), to examine the rehabilitation policy of the project and suggest further measures, improvements, etc. The HRC submitted its recommendations to the government in November 1997. The government of India, after examining the recommendations of the HRC, accepted certain additional benefits/measures, which were incorporated in the rehabilitation policy of 1998.

The major recommendations of the Hanumantha Rao Committee, approved by the government in regard to rehabilitation of the affected population, include the definition of *family* so as to make all major sons and major daughters who attained the age of 21 years and dependent parent (mother/father) of the fully affected entitled landowner as on 19 July 1990 eligible for ex-gratia payment of Rs. 33,000/-, i.e. 750 days minimum agricultural wage each, grant of house construction assistance to the urban landowner families, linked with the progress of construction and shifting, allotment of one constructed shop, recognition of the right of the people living in the villages upstream of the Tehri reservoir, over the water from Bhagirathi and Bhilangana rivers and tributaries for drinking and irrigation purposes.

Improvements after Government Decision on HRC (2001)

Additional measures/benefits agreed after HRC:

Rural

- Minimum amount of cash in lieu of land allotment, equivalent to the cost of 2 acres of allotted land, has increased from Rs. 2 lakh to Rs. 5 lakh.
- House construction assistance to fully affected rural house owners whose land/house has been acquired is given at Rs. 1 lakh each.
- Cash grants admissible for shifting and purchase of seeds and fertilizers are increased.
- Eligibility criteria for land allotment: GoUP orders of 1976/78 to stand modified so as to make eligible for land allotment those landowners in rural area who sold their part land after 1978 but before the issue of section 4(1) notification under Land Acquisition Act.
- Rural shopkeepers are to be paid cash compensation at Rs. 60,000 each to those having shops on national highways or other highways and large market areas, and at Rs. 40,000 each to shopkeepers on other roads in submergence areas.

Urban

- Amount of house construction assistance was revised, varying from Rs. 2.5 lakh to Rs. 4.5 lakh, depending on the plot size.

- The cost of flats and shops were allotted to the entitled oustees to be recovered at pre-1989 construction cost (development cost not to be charged).
- The government of Uttaranchal allowed in July 2001 the payment of cash grant to shopkeepers of Old Tehri Town, ranging from Rs. 1 lakh to Rs. 3 lakh, depending on the category of the shop, subject to handing over possession of their shop.
- The government of Uttaranchal, in December 2001, allowed the payment of cash grant of Rs. 1.5 lakh each to the advocates of Old Tehri Town who were practising before the year 1985.

Additional Measures Agreed by GoI for Public Facilities and Infrastructure Development (2005)

- Enhancement of compensation for rural shopkeepers from the existing Rs. 40,000 to Rs. 80,000 for shopkeepers at other roads and Rs. 60,000 to for Rs. 1,20,000 for shopkeepers at national highways or other highways.
- Reconstruction and reallocation of public properties situated below EL 835 m in partially submerged villages at a higher level for population residing above submergence level.
- The arrangement of ferry boat/cable car services for cut-off area
- Heavy-motor-vehicle bridge across Bhagirathi River near village Dobra, with funding to be provided by the government of Uttaranchal and the government of India.

Table 3.1 Resettlement and Rehabilitation Policies of Various Projects

type of PAFs	Tungabhadra	Bhakra	Ukai	Srisailam	Tehri	Sardar Sarovar	Indira Sagar and Maheshwar
Landed family	5–10 acres of agricultural land free of cost.	There was no information available on R & R package. - PAPs were paid cash compensation.	Land made available was 0.1 to 4 acres, depending on the land acquired. The land was sold to oustees at Rs. 600–960.	50% of compensation subject to a maximum of Rs. 1,000 per acre for the land acquired. 50% compensation subject Rs. 5,000 paid where land and house were acquired.	2 acres of irrigated land or cash of Rs. 5 lakh in lieu of land.	Minimum of 2 ha. land for agricultural purpose.	2–8 ha. 50% compensation, and the remaining 50% adjusted against the cost on the allotted land to be recovered in 20 years.
Major sons	-	-	-	-	No provision.	2 ha. for agricultural purpose.	Treated as separate family. Only cash compensation.
Co-sharer	-	-	-	-	-	2 ha. for agricultural purpose.	No provision.
Major unmarried daughter	-	-	-	-	No provision.	No provision.	No provision.
Widows	-	-	-	-	No provision.	No provision.	No provision.

	Tungabhadra	Bhakra	Ukai	Srisailam	Tehri	Sardar Sarovar	Indira Sagar and Maheshwar
Encroachers	-	-	-	-	Urban PAFs provision exists.	2 ha. prior to one year of notification.	Entitled to compensation.
Landless PAFs	-	-	-	-	2 acres for agricultural land.	2 ha. to agricultural labourers.	a. No land. b. Rs. 29,000 for SC/ST. c. Rs. 19,500 to others.
House	a) 700 sq. m land for house and other purposes. b) 185–200% of ex-gratia at market value of house. c) Housing construction material at subsidized rates.	-	3200 sq. ft for landowners and 1600 sq. ft to those who do not own land. Compensation to house was paid.	50% of compensation subject to a maximum of Rs. 1000 where house was acquired.	200 sq. m land at nominal rate of Rs. 330 minimum compensation of Rs. 1 lakh.	a. 500 sq. m free of cost cash compensation for submerged land. b. Rs. 10,000 per family to construct pucca house.	Plot of 5,400 sq. ft free to oustees and their major son and compensation as per LA Act or Rs. 20,000 in lieu of plot.

	Tungabhadra	Bhakra	Ukai	Srisailam	Tehri	Sardar Sarovar	Indira Sagar and Maheshwar
Partially affected families	-	-	-	-	Provision of Rs. 20,000 worth of IGS scheme for those who are left with less than 1.5 ha. and Rs. 5,000 for those who are left with more than 1.5 ha. land.	No provision.	No provision.
Employment	-	Gainful employment was provided.	-		Preference in employment.	Preference in employment.	Not mentioned.
Rehabilitation grant	Free transport provided to displaced persons.	Rs. 250 per family was provided.	-	Weaker sections were provided houses and house sites and hutment charges of Rs. 1,000 on humanitarian grounds. Others were allotted house sites on payment at market value for land.	Shifting grant: Rs. 5,000. Intensive shifting within prescribed time: Rs. 15,000. Urban shifting grant: Rs. 3,000–4000. Intensive shifting grant within prescribed time: Rs. 12,000.	a. Rs. 15 per day for 25 days. b. Rs. 754 per family. c. Grant in aid up to Rs. 500.	a. Rehabilitation grant of Rs. 18,700 to landless, small and marginal, and SC/ST families. b. Others: Rs. 9,350.

	Tungabhadra	Bhakra	Ukai	Srisailam	Tehri	Sardar Sarovar	Indira Sagar and Maheshwar
House/building advance/loan	-	Assistance to construct house.	Rs. 4,000–5,000 at 7% interest. Those who did not opt for government help were offered Rs. 450–670 for cooperating with the government.	-	Up to 1 lakh at subsidized interest.	No provision.	No provision.
Facilities affected due to the construction of project colony and project work	-	-	-	-	Entitled for rehabilitation benefits.	-	No provision.
Subsistence allowance	-	-	-	-	-	Rs. 4,500 per family.	
Grant for purchase of productive assets	-	-	-	-	-	Rs. 7,000 per family.	a. Rs. 49,300 for landless agricultural labour. b. Rs. 33,150 for others.
Insurance	-	-	-	-	-	For hut, death, loss of limbs, disablement.	-

Sources:

1. Data collected from various projects.

2. 'Report of the Expert Committee on Rehabilitation and Environmental Aspects of THDC', vol. 2, annexure, Oct. 1997.

3.4 Administrative Set-Up under the State Government

The Tehri dam project was being implemented by the Irrigation Department of the government of Uttar Pradesh till 1989. The commissioner (Garhwal division) was notified as the administrator of the project, looking after the rehabilitation and other related activities, under which the rehabilitation wing was constituted. The following is the administrative wing:

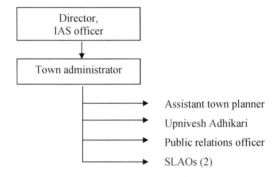

The above officers were assisted by the supporting staff as per the sanctioned strength. In addition, the PWD division with staff and irrigation division with staff were also working under the administrator. A high-level control board was constituted under the chairmanship of the chief minister of UP for economic and efficient expedition of implementation. Under this control board, a standing committee was formed to monitor physical and financial progress. The control board also assisted the state government in framing the policies for rehabilitation and other aspects by laying down guidelines.

Monitoring Mechanism for Rehabilitation

The government of India has constituted a project-level monitoring committee (PLMC) for conducting field visits to verify the satisfactory completion of various environmental safeguards stipulated at the time of project clearance and other specific recommendations accepted by the government. The committee comprises of the Regional Chief Conservator of Forests, representatives of the Ministry of Environment and Forests, Ministry of Power, Jawaharlal Nehru University, and Indian Agricultural Research Institute. The committee also includes independent experts and an NGO.

The Ministry of Environment and Forests (government of India) also constituted a high-level inter-ministerial review committee headed by the secretary of MOEF to periodically review the environment and rehabilitation and resettlement issues associated with the Tehri hydroelectric project and also to review the recommendations of the project-level monitoring committee. The committee comprises of the following:

1. Secretary, Ministry of Environment and Forests - chairman
2. Secretary, Ministry of Power - member
3. Secretary, Ministry of Social Justice - member
4. Secretary, Ministry of Water Resources - member

Chief secretaries of the governments of Uttar Pradesh and Uttaranchal are special invitees.

Grievance Redressal Mechanism

A grievance redressal cell under the director (rehabilitation), who is also the district magistrate, Tehri, is functioning in the Rehabilitation Directorate, Uttaranchal government, for expeditious disposal of grievances received from PAFs. Further, coordination committee headed by the commissioner (Garhwal), set up by the state government, also redresses the specific cases/demands of the people.

3.5 Overall Status of R & R

Urban Rehabilitation

The Old Tehri Town (OTT), comprised of urban population of 5,291 families categorized as fully affected, has been completely rehabilitated at the New Tehri Town (NTT) or in Haridwar or Dehradun districts as per the option of the oustees (table 3.2).

Table 3.2 Status of Rehabilitation of PAFs of Old Tehri Town

Description	Required	Constructed/ Developed	Allotted	Percentage Allotted (Progress)
1. Residences				
a. Plots	2,438	2,438	2,438	100%
b. Flats	2,853	2,853	2,728	100%
Total (a and b)	5,291	5,291	5,166	100%
2. Commercial				
Shops	784	787	787	100%

- All the eligible persons have been given rehabilitation benefits.

The NTT is at a height of 1,350 to 1,850 m, overlooking the lake, with a panoramic view of the Himalayas. The new township has all the modern facilities for education (including ITI and a university), 75-bedded hospital, financial institutions, district administration offices, markets, a bus stand, and places of worship, etc. The Old Tehri Town has been vacated in January 2004.

Rural Rehabilitation

All the 3,355 fully affected rural families in the villages have been rehabilitated through the allotment of land/cash compensation. In partially affected villages, out of 2,074 fully affected rural families, 1,620 families have been rehabilitated. There were 5,429 rural families which have been categorized as fully affected families and another 3,810 rural families as partially affected. Rural resettlement colonies are located in Dehradun and Haridwar districts and have been provided with all civic facilities (table 3.3).

Table 3.3 Status of Rehabilitation in Rural Areas

S. No.	Description	Land Affected (in Acre)	No. of Villages	Fully Affected Families	Rehabilitation Facilities Provided	Balance PAFs
1	Fully submerged/ affected villages	2,993.93	37	3,355	3,355	–
2	Partially submerged/ affected villages	1,936.91	72	2,074	1,620	454
	Total	4,930.84	109	5,429	4,975	454

The partially affected families, about 3,810 in number, were not relocated but given cash compensation. Out of 3,810 partially affected families, 2,280 were paid cash, and the rest were under process. All R & R benefits have been paid up to EL 790 m, and affected families resettled. Disbursement of compensation/grants between EL 790 m and 835 m was completed.

Transfer of Facilities

All public properties/community facilities created under the project have been transferred to concerned departments of the state government. It was also decided that the concerned departments should make their own budgetary provision for operation and maintenance of the properties/community facilities, and no further expenditure shall be incurred by the project for the same.

Connectivity and Public Facilities in Cut-Off Area

- In lieu of Tehri–Dharasu road, Chamba–Dharasu road at higher altitude was constructed at project cost.
- In lieu of Tehri–Ghansali road, Tehri-Bhagirathipuram-Tipri-Ghansali road was constructed at project cost.
- Two medium-motor-vehicle suspension bridges have been constructed, one each in Bhagirathi and Bhilangana valley at a cost of Rs. 30

crores. While Pipal Dali MMV bridge on Bhilangana has been opened for the traffic, Siyansu MMV bridge is expected to be made operational soon after completion of the connecting approach roads. However, the pedestrians have been allowed to cross the bridge.

- Meanwhile, ferry services have been provided at the project cost till such time the bridge and its approach roads are completed to facilitate the people living in cut-off areas.

- Additional package of Rs. 25 crores for road connectivity with bridges, reconstruction and relocation of public facilities below 835 m at higher elevation for the use of the population residing above submergence level, arrangement of cable car and ferry-boat for cut-off area, and enhancement of competition for rural shopkeepers of cut-off area has been provided.

- A heavy-motor-vehicle bridge across Bhagirathi River near village Dobra with a span of 532 m (5.5 m clear roadway for single lane), amounting to Rs. 90 crores, is also being constructed with funding by GoUK and GoI. As decided in the meeting held by the honourable minister of power on 19 September 2006, an ad hoc advance of Rs. 20 crores has been released by THDC to GoUK for the construction of the bridge.

- In the meeting held by the honourable minister of power on 19 September 2006, it was felt that an arrangement of a barrage with the capability to carry load be explored and implemented urgently. It was noted that since the water level in the reservoir varies up to 90 m, the operation of barrage in such conditions would entail an appropriate system of jetties at both ends, i.e. floating jetties.

- As discussed in the meeting held by the honourable minister of power on 22 November 2006, the ferry arrangements are to be made operational in around six months' time. Order has been placed by THDC on WAPCOS on 14 December 2006 for the consultancy services for floating jetties/ferry specification. WAPCOS is preparing feasibility report in the first instance.

Rehabilitation and Resettlement Sites

The rural resettlement colonies are located in agricultural areas in Dehradun and Haridwar districts and have been provided with all civic facilities, like electricity, irrigation, piped drinking water, roads, schools, dispensaries, places of worships, and community centres.

Cost/Expenditure of R & R

Demands are being raised for additional funds for rehabilitation work at different forums by various leaders. The approved provision for R & R as per revised cost estimates was Rs. 983.14 crores (in March 2003 price level). With additional measures agreed by government, expenditure on rehabilitation is likely to be around Rs. 1,260 crores. An expenditure of Rs. 1,231.56 crores (provisional) has already been incurred.

Table 3.4 Status of Rehabilitation of PAFs of Oil Tehri Town

S. No.	Description of Affected Family	Total No. of PAFs	Shifting Status from Old Tehri			
			Shifted	Balance	Progress	
1	Landowner, benap house owner, father's land, etc. (as per 1985 survey)	3,001	3,001	Nil	100%	All PAFs and unauthorized families have evacuated Old Tehri Town.
2	Government/semi-government employees, tenants, etc. (excluding labourers and unauthorized families)	2,290	2,290	Nil	100%	
	Total	5,291	5,291	Nil	100%	

All 5,291 PAFs (population about 20,000), including landowners, tenants, shopkeepers, Kokha, Thelidharak, labours, hawkers, and unauthorized families, have been given property compensation, plots/flats, shops, and rehabilitation grants (table 3.4). A few unsettled/disputed claims (i.e. house construction assistance), ex-gratia and leftover property claims, etc. are still under process.

Status of Rural Rehabilitation (up to RL 835 m)

There are 109 villages (37 fully submerged and 72 partially submerged) in the submergence of Tehri dam. Total 5,187 entitled families have been resettled/ allotted plots in new resettlement sites. All the families residing between RL 790 m and RL 835 m have been allotted land at new resettlement sites (table 3.5).

The 3,810 partially affected rural families are not to be relocated but are paid cash compensation for their part of land coming under submergence. Since land was scare in Tehri district, rural families have been resettled in Dehradun and Haridwar districts. For rural displaced families (including landless labourers), two acres of developed irrigated land per family (or half acre if resettlement site is within urban municipal limit) was provided at new resettlement sites. New resettlement colonies for rural PAFs are Pashulok near Rishikesh, Raiwala, Bhaniyawala, Banjarawala, Parwal, Central Hope Town, West Hope Town, Fulsani in Dehradun district, and Pathri block, Pathri Rao, Roshnabad in Haridwar district.

Table 3.5 Progress of Rural Rehabilitation (up to FRL 835 m)

S. No.	Description	Land Affected (in Acre)	No. of Villages	Fully Affected Families	Rehabilitation Facilities Provided	Progress
1	Fully submerged/ affected villages	2,993.93	37	3,355	3,355	100%
2	Partially submerged/ affected villages	1,936.91	72	1,832	1,832	100%
	Total	4,930.84	109	5,187	5,187	100%

- The 3,810 partially affected families are not relocated, but cash compensation was paid. Out of 3,810 households, 2,510 have been paid cash, and the rest is under process.
- The fully affected families identified so far have been allocated land in the new resettlement sites along with due compensation. Only 454 families are residing between RL 790 m and RL 835 m.

- Survey of India has been deployed for marking of final contour line at RL 835 m along the periphery of reservoir to identify the final left-out families and land/properties of PAFs, if any.

Rehabilitation Plan for Balance Rural PAFs

Balance rural families, if identified after the survey of RL 835 m by Survey of India, are proposed to be rehabilitated, as given in table 3.6.

Table 3.6 Proposed Rehabilitation of Balance Rural Families (RL 835 m)

S. No.	Name of Rehabilitation Site	No. of Families
1	Virbhadra, Pashulok, etc. in Dehradun district	35
2	Pathri block, Haridwar district	15
3	Pathri Rao (Suman nagar), Haridwar district	45
4	Shivalik nagar in Haridwar district	9
5	Roshnabad in Haridwar district	27
	Total	132

Table 3.7 Details of Funds Received and Expenditure for Rehabilitation Work

S. No.	Fin. Year	Received from THDC	From Oustees	From Government of UK	Total	Expenditure	Balance
1	2000–01	522,975,881	4,263,453.09		527,239,334	507,303,651	
2	2001–02	1,152,000,000	45,149,652.7	150,000,000	1,347,149,653	1,323,852,327	
3	2002–03	1,753,000,000	16,265,465.9		1,769,265,466	1,796,236,687	
4	2003–04	753,000,000	5,726,026.5		758,726,027	756,391,099	
5	2004–05	620,000,000	12,707,678.6	10,000,000	642,707,679	613,441,857	
6	2005–06	1,435,715,000	6,791,724	100,000,000	1,542,506,724	1,145,531,783	
7	2006–07	769,400,000	2,237,124		771,637,124	833,734,261	
		7,006,090,881	93,141,124.8	260,000,000	7,359,232,006	6,976,491,664	382,740,341
					5,180,000,000	5,180,000,000	
	.				12,539,232,006	12,156,491,664	382,740,342

Balance fund with Rehabilitation Directorate = Rs. 38.27 crores.

Balance of funds will be utilized as follows:

1. Construction of Dobra–Chanti HMV bridge: Rs. 20.00 crores
2. Construction of ropeway for cut-off area, payment of balance properties in submergence area, and development work in resettlement areas: Rs. 18.27 crores
3. Cost of construction of Dobra–Chanti HMV bridge: Rs. 89.20 crores
4. Released fund against Dobra–Chanti HMV bridge: Rs. 31.00 crores (Rs. 11.00 crores from the government of UK + Rs. 20.00 crores from THDC/GoI)
5. Balance funds: Rs. 58.20 crores
6. Demand of special package for affected/cut-off areas of Tehri dam project: Rs. 248.00 crores.

3.6 Description of Sample Villages of Rehabilitation Sites of THDC

Under rural segment, ten villages were covered from two districts (six villages were covered in Dehradun district and four villages were covered in Haridwar district). The villages covered under rural segment were Pashulok, Banjarawala, Bhaniawala, Dehrakhas, Raiwala, and Attak Farm in the Dehradun district and Pathri block 1, Pathri block 2, Pathri block 3 and Pathri Rao/Suman nagar in the Haridwar district. The urban rehabilitation centre covered under the urban segment was New Tehri Town, which includes Baurari and Mooldhar (including tin-shed areas).

The rehabilitation colonies were located in the major districts—namely, Haridwar, Rishikesh, and Dehradun. Some of them are near the towns, and some others in the interior areas. The number of households rehabilitated in these settlements is not uniform. Some are more dependent on agriculture, while some are more urbanized locations. The sex ratio varies—927 females per 1,000 males in Attak Farm and 995 females to 1,000 males in Banjarawala. The literacy rate in these colonies is more than 74%.

The facilities offered by the THDC for these rehabilitated colonies are safe drinking water, with the construction of one overhead tank and pipeline, irrigation canals/channels for agriculture, metalled road, panchayat office, temple, shops, school, dispensary/primary health centre, and electricity facility with erected LT line.

The PAPs constructed their houses in a modern way, with sophisticated furnishings with the compensation received from THDC, and purchased vehicles for their private transport. The irrigation facility was made available to the farmers to grow short-term high-yielding verities of crops, like vegetables, fruits, sugar cane, paddy, wheat, and sweetcorn. The public transport system is also made available in the area, which helps to transport their agricultural produce to the local markets easily, economically, and timely. The PAPs in the colonies are enjoying all types of facilities, like entertainment, education, health, shopping, and financial institutions, because most of the sites are closely located to the state capital and other urban centres and these sites are chosen themselves by PAFs. The opportunity of employment has increased. The details of the facilities provided in these colonies are provided in annexure 3.1.

Some of the major observations about the rehabilitated sites are:

> The new settlements are provided with water, electricity, and other basic amenities.
> Both primary and secondary schools are near to the villages.
> Most sites are nearby town, enhancing the new opportunities for employment for youth.
> The status of women has increased both at the village and at home.
> Social fabric of the PAFs is intact as they moved in group.

Major complaints of the people in these colonies are:

> Traditional sources of employment are reduced.
> Agricultural support services like markets and extension services are not reached.
> In suburban sites, most of the time, the allotted half-acre land is not able to utilize for optimum use by the PAFs.
> Some sites are situated in low-lying areas, which require proper drainage facilities.
> Some rehabilitation sites are located in interior areas which are adjacent to forest areas and need to be provided with streetlights.

New Tehri Town

NTT is developed by the THDC on the top of the hill exclusively to rehabilitate the Tehri-dam-affected urban PAPs. The total number of households in NTT is 5,476. The total population is 25,423. The literacy rate is 85.86%.

The facilities provided by the THDC for this rehabilitated colony are safe drinking-water facility with water supply distribution system, well-connected blacktop road network, comprehensive sewerage system, 75-bedded hospital, educational institutions (including university campus), shopping complexes/shops, good electric lines with consistent power supply, high-mast street lighting, religious places, bus stand, stadium, multipurpose hall, veterinary hospital, good communications systems (including posts and telegraphs), financial institutions, parks, police station, public distribution system/ration shops, fuel (like gas, kerosene, petrol, and diesel) and other necessary infrastructure.

The Tehri-dam-affected PAPs constructed some of the houses, and the rest were constructed by the THDC. The construction was not uniform. Some constructed their houses in a modern way. The important occupation in the NTT is employment and business. Unlike in Old Tehri Town, in NTT the public transport system is very efficient. It enhanced accessibility to all basic amenities and recreation facilities for entertainment, education, health, shopping, financial institutions, etc. even though physical distance is more due to uneven terrain. The opportunity of employment has increased for both men and women in non-traditional sources.

The problems faced by the PAPs of the NTT are dwindling of traditional sources of employment and markets, being cut off from other places for trade, and bad weather because the NTT was constructed on a higher altitude.

Major areas of dissatisfaction of the people:

- ➢ Ownership of allotted houses in tin shed should be transferred to the people.
- ➢ Employment opportunities to be increased by encouraging local resource-based small-scale industries.
- ➢ The cost of living has been increased, and there is a need for effective public distribution system.
- ➢ Tax incentives to be given to shop owners and small industrial units.
- ➢ Poor grievance redressal system.

➢ Very long and cumbersome procedures for compensation allotment.

➢ Cases that are still pending in THDC.

➢ Business opportunities are low when compared to OTT.

➢ Tin-shed colonies to be improved with basic amenities, schools, and children's park.

➢ Major government offices are scattered very far away.

➢ Tehri dam reservoir to be used in many ways to reduce drinking water scarcity, employment through large-scale fishing, boating tourism, etc.

➢ Shops are provided in unsuitable locality/place, creating hurdle in business.

Annexure 3.1

Details of Facilities Created at Various Resettlement Centres for Oustees of Tehri (Stage 1)

S. No.	Name of Resettlement Centre	Facilities Created	Present Status
	Urban		
1	New Tehri Town	i. roads	Transferred to concerned department.
		ii. sewerage system	- do -
		iii. street lighting	- do -
		iv. religious building	- do -
		v. bus stand	- do -
		vi. stadium and multipurpose hall	- do -
		vii. hospital: 75–bedded	- do -
		viii. university campus	- do -
		ix. water supply distribution system	Yet to be transferred.
2	Ajabpur Kala (Dehradun district)	i. drinking water scheme (1 OH tank + 3 km pipeline)	Completed
		ii. metalled road (3.30 km)	-do.-
		iii. temple (1), shops (17), and business centre (1)	-do.-
		iv. LT line (3.30 km)	Transferred to concerned department.
	Rural **A. Facilities Completed**		
1	Bhaniawala (Dehradun district)	i. tube wells (9)	Transferred to Irrigation Department (tube-well division).
		ii. drinking water scheme (2 OH tank + 35.7 km pipeline)	Transferred to Garhwal Jal Sasthan.
		iii. metalled road (31 km)	Transferred to the Rural Energy Department.
		iv. irrigation guls (44 km)	Transferred to concerned department.

		v. LT line (26 km)	- do -
		vi. schools (8)	- do -
		vii. panchayat ghar (3)	- do -
		viii. community hall/shops (10), shopping complex	- do -
		ix. temples (4)	- do -
		x. primary health centre, post office, veterinary hospital, seed store, kanji house, etc.	- do - -do.-
2	Raiwala (Dehradun district)	i. drinking water scheme (1 OH tank and 10 km pipeline)	
		ii. irrigation guls (10 km)	Transferred to concerned department.
		iii. metalled road (8 km)	-do
		iv. primary health centre	-do.
		v. panchayat ghar (2) and dormitory (1)	-do.
		vi. temple (2)	-do.
		vii. LT line (8 km)	Transferred to concerned department.
		viii. primary school (1)	- do -
3	Attak Farm (Dehradun district)	i. roads (5.5 km)	Transferred to concerned department
		ii. irrigation facilities tube well (1) irrigation gul (3.30 km)	-do.
		iii. drinking-water facilities (1 OH tank and 1.50 km pipeline)	-do-
		iv. electrification (3.20 km LT line)	-do-
4	Banjarawala (Dehradun district)	i. drinking water scheme (1 OH tank + 3.5 km pipeline)	Transferred to concerned department
		ii. irrigation gul (9.4 km)	-do.-
		iii. metalled road (13 km)	-do.-
		iv. panchayat ghar (1), temple (1), shops (2), primary school (1), dispensary (1)	-do-
		v. LT line (5 km)	Transferred to concerned department.
		vi. primary health centre	- do -

5	Parwal (Dehradun district)	i. roads (3.50 km)	Transferred to concerned department
		ii. irrigation facilities 1 tube well 3.30 km irrigation gul	-d0.-
		iii. drinking-water facilities (2 km pipeline)	-do.-
		iv. electrification (5 km LT line)	-do.-
6	Dehrakhas (Dehradun district)	i. drinking water scheme (1 OH tank and 6 km pipeline)	Transferred to concerned department
		ii. metalled road (5 km)	-do-
		iii. panchayat ghar (1)	-do-
		iv. irrigation gul (3 km)	-do-
		v. LT line (4 km)	-do-
7	Pathri block 1 (Haridwar district)	i. roads (25 km)	Transferred to concerned department
		ii. irrigation facilities (4 tube wells and 16 irrigation guls)	-do.-
		iii. drinking-water facilities (1 OH tank and 3 km pipeline)	-do.-
		iv. electrification (7 km LT line)	do
		v. Schools 1 primary school 1 high school	do
		vi. panchayat ghar (1)	-do.
		vii. community hall (1)	-do.
		viii. shopping complex (2) and shop (8)	-do.
		ix. temples (2)	do.
		x. primary health centre (1)	-do.
		xi. post office (1)	-do.
		xii. veterinary hospital (1)	-do.
		xiv. seed store (1)	-do.
		xv. bus stop (2)	-do.

8	Pathri Rao (Haridwar)	i. drinking water scheme (1 OH tank + 2.80 km pipeline)	Transferred to concerned department
		ii. metalled road (19 km)	-do.
		iii. irrigation gul (14 km) and tube wells (3)	-do.
		iv. LT line (7 km)	Transferred to concerned department.
		v. primary school/junior high school (1 each)	-do.
		vi. temple (1)	-do.
		vii. primary health centre and veterinary hospital (1 each)	-do.
		viii. shops (8) and dormitory (1)	-do.
		ix. post office/police chowki (1 each)	-do.
9	Shivalik Nagar (Haridwar)	i. irrigation gul (4 km) and tube well (1)	Transferred to concerned department
		ii. LT line (2 km)	-do.
		iii. metalled road (5 km)	-do.
		iv. panchayat ghar/dormitory (1 each)	-do.
		v. primary health centre (1)	-do.
		vi. post office (1)	-do.
	Rural B. Facilities under Execution		
1	Pathri block 2	i. irrigation facilities tube well (6) irrigation guls (8.50 km)	Transferred to concerned department
		ii. drinking-water facilities (1 OH tank and 9 km pipelines)	-do.-
		iii. electrification work	-do.
		iv. community facility primary school (1) panchayat ghar (3) temples (3) shops (10) dormitories (50)	-do.
		v. roads (31 km)	-do.

2	Pathri block 3	i. irrigation facilities tube well (10) irrigation guls (24 km)	Transferred to concerned department
		ii. drinking-water facilities (2 OH tank and 6 km pipelines)	-do.
		iii. electrification work 11 KV line: 5 km LT line: 9 km	-do.
		iv. community facility primary school (1) panchayat ghar (3) temples (3) shops (20) dormitories (20)	-do.
		v. roads (43 km)	-do.
3	Pathri block 4	i. irrigation facilities tube wells (3) irrigation guls (14 km)	Transferred to concerned department
		ii. drinking-water facilities (1 OH tank and 2.8 km pipeline)	-do.
		iii. LT line: 7 km	-do.
		iv. community facility 1 primary school and 1 junior high school 1 panchayat ghar 1 veterinary hospital 1 post office 8 shops 1 dormitory	-do.
		v. roads (19 km)	-do.
4	Suman nagar	i. irrigation facilities tube well (1) irrigation guls (3 km)	Transferred to concerned department
		ii. drinking-water facilities (1 OH tank and 1.5 km pipeline)	-do.
		iii. electrification work 11 KV line: 7.50 km LT line: 1.50 km	-do.
		iv. community facility 1 temple 2 shops 1 dormitory	-do.
		v. roads (1.50 km)	-do.

Chapter 4

Social Status of Households

This chapter describes the social status of the households rehabilitated in the project area. As mentioned earlier, 150 households in urban areas and 200 in rural areas were covered for intensive field survey.

Out of 350 households surveyed, 92% belong to Hindus, and about 8% belong to Muslims. Though other communities are there, they constitute about 0.3% (graph 4.1). Interestingly, all the rural households belong to Hindus, and about 81% in urban areas are Hindus. Among Hindus, proportion of Rajputs is highest (38% of population), followed by Garhwali (24%), and Brahmin (23%) respectively. Garhwali and Rajputs constitute about 80% of the households in rural areas. It indicates that overall upper-caste population is higher among resettled population (table 4.2).

Graph 4.1 Religion-Wise Distribution of Household

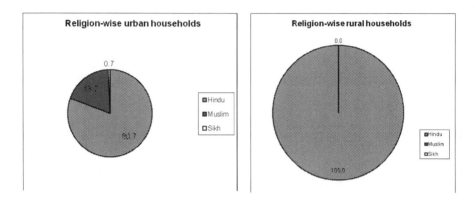

Temple at New Tehri Town.

Table 4.2 Caste-Wise Distribution of Household

Caste	Urban	Rural	Total
Amsur	2.1	0.0	1.2
Balmiki	4.2	0.0	2.4
Brahmin	27.1	17.6	23.2
Chauhan	2.1	0.0	1.2
Garhwali	12.5	41.2	24.4
Jain	2.1	0.0	1.2
Lauhar	2.1	0.0	1.2
Rajput	37.5	38.2	37.8
SC	2.1	0.0	1.2
Shah	2.1	0.0	1.2
Sikh	2.1	0.0	1.2
Srawan	2.1	0.0	1.2
Vaish aggarwal	2.1	0.0	1.2
Panwar	0.0	2.9	1.2
Total	100.0 (150)	100.0 (200)	100.0 (350)

For most of the urban resettlers who shifted from OTT to NTT, the distance between previous residence and resettlement sites is between 11 km and 30 km. For rural resettlers, this distance is higher as they are relocated to villages in Haridwar and Dehradun (table 4.3). About 82% of resettlers of rural population are shifted to more than 100 km from their previous settlements. However, the unique character of resettlement policy of Tehri is that displaced population has been given the chance to choose their resettlement locations. As a result, the social fabric of the relocating village population from resettlement colonies as a whole has not been disturbed due to rehabilitation.

Bus stand at New Tehri Town.

Table 4.3 Distance of Displacement from the Previous Residence of Household

Distance in Kilometres	Urban	Rural	Total
≤10	0.0	0.0	0.0
11–20	37.3	0.0	16.0
21–30	57.3	0.0	24.6
31–50	5.3	0.0	2.3
51–75	0.0	0.0	0.0
76–100	0.0	17.5	10.0
>100	0.0	82.5	47.1
Total	100.0 (150)	100.0 (200)	100.0 (350)

Among the total households, landowners comprised about 57%, followed by persons who are having land on their father's name (26%), and about 11% are tenants. Most of the landowners are based in rural areas, while tenants and PAFs who did have land on their father's name are based in urban areas (graph 4.2). As the focus of the study is mainly on fully affected households, in the sample, about 92% households are fully affected—out of which 85.5% from rural areas and 100% from urban areas (graph 4.3). However, the sample represents all categories of households, viz. resettlers who came from partially submerged areas along with their relatives, households relocated in the construction of NTT, Pariyojana colony, and project office. This represents all sections of the rehabilitated population. All urban resettlers from OTT are fully submerged and resettled at NTT.

Graph 4.2 Distribution of Category of Affected Family

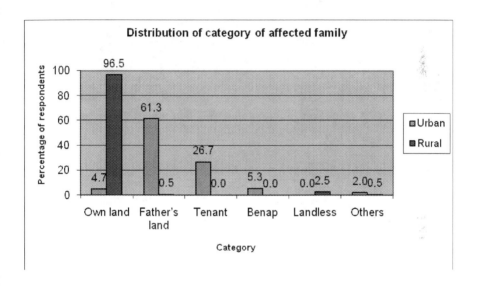

Government hospital at New Tehri Town.

Graph 4.3 Details of Submerged Area

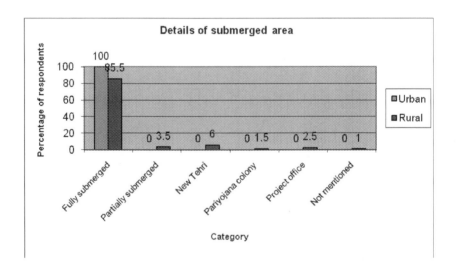

Age-wise distribution of households shows that majority of the population are in the age group of 21–30 years (23%), followed by 31–40 years (18%), and then

41–50 years (12%) (graph 4.4). The age profile of rural and urban households is almost similar for all age groups. This indicates that most of the rehabilitated are relatively young and capable of making adjustments with the new situation and able to take advantage of new opportunities coming out of rehabilitation and resettlement.

Graph 4.4 Age-Wise Distribution of Households

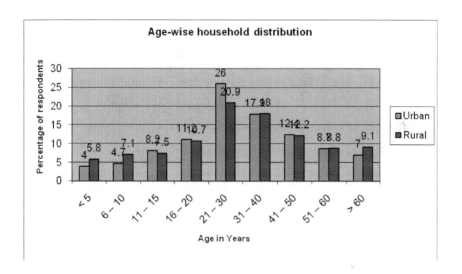

The average size of households is 5.3 in urban areas, while it is 5.4 in case of rural households. The sex ratio of the sample households is 892 in case of urban households, while in the case of rural households, it is still low (800). Overall sex ratio is about 862, which indicates unfavourable gender situation among households for women, particularly among rural households (graph 4.5). Overall, the percentage of persons who are educated up to high school and above has marginally increased from 76% to 77% after rehabilitation compared to before rehabilitation (table 4.8) as most of the resettlement sites are situated in suburban/urban areas. In urban areas, percentage of persons educated up to 10+2, graduates, and postgraduates increased significantly, while in rural areas, the percentage of high school educated and graduates increased significantly. This indicates that the facilities for higher education were more in resettlement sites compared to previous locations. However, there is no significant reduction in illiteracy; it may be due to high birth rate and increase in children below 7 years in the population.

Graph 4.5 Gender-Wise Distribution of Households

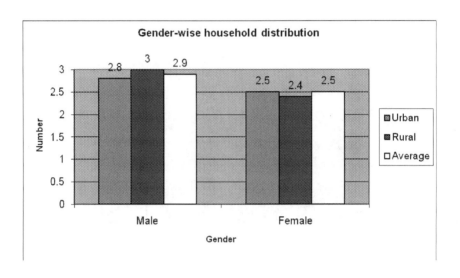

Table 4.8 Distribution of Education of Households before and after Displacement

	Urban		Rural		Total	
	Before Displacement	After Displacement	Before Displacement	After Displacement	Before Displacement	After Displacement
Illiterate	3.8	6.5	3.0	2.9	3.4	4.6
Primary	12.7	9.3	18.3	17.8	15.6	13.7
Secondary	5.6	4.1	3.7	5.0	4.6	4.6
High school	26.3	20.8	29.4	35.0	27.9	28.1
College education	13.8	17.2	23.8	18.0	19.0	17.6
Graduation	18.5	21.5	1.3	16.3	9.6	18.8
Post graduation	14.0	16.5	16.1	3.7	15.1	9.9
Professional	5.4	4.1	4.4	1.3	4.9	2.7
Total	100.0 (150)	100.0 (150)	100.0 (200)	100.0 (200)	100.0 (350)	100.0 (350)

From Homelessness to House Reconstruction

Throughout the world, resettlers tend to display a strong propensity to improve their living standards over the past levels. They do so through incremental investments in kind (labour) and cash. With the need for shelter and the aspiration for better living standards, resettlers often look for larger and more durable homes. Most of the PAPs in the rural and urban areas have constructed their houses in a modern way with sophisticated furnishings using the compensation they received from the THDC.

Graph 4.6 Distribution of Nature of the House of Household

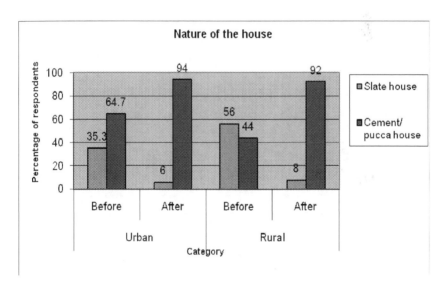

Residence of a sample household.

A home not only can give protection from different weather conditions, but it can also provide comfortable resting and sleeping for poverty-stricken people. For this, the THDC has given a one-room flat to the economically weaker homeless oustees at free of cost in the rehabilitated area.

About half of the households (35% of the urban households and 56% of the rural households) were living in the slate houses, and the remaining half of them were living in cement/pucca houses before displacement (graph 4.6). The number of households living in the cement/pucca houses has increased tremendously up to 93% after the rehabilitation. In urban areas, households with cement/pucca houses increased from 65% to 94%, whereas in rural areas, households with cement/pucca houses increased from 44% to 92%. This is a very significant positive development after the rehabilitation (graph 4.6). Households whose houses was in lesser value before rehabilitation have moved to higher-value houses as THDC provided/helped the PAPs to construct pucca houses (table 4.10). Many of the households have constructed modern houses near the urban centres, and their value increased by leaps and bounds.

Table 4.10 Distribution of Value of the House of the Respondent before and after Displacement

(Rs.)

	Before Displacement				After Displacement			
	Urban		Rural		Urban		Rural	
	Slate House	Cement/ Pucca House	Slate House	Cement/ Pucca House	Slate House	Cement/ Pucca House	Slate House	Cement/ Pucca House
Up to 50,000	37.7	17.9	51.2	22.7	50.0	9.1	0.0	3.3
50,001–100,000	13.2	13.7	33.1	36.4	50.0	12.6	0.0	3.3
100,001–150,000	0.0	3.2	2.3	3.4	0.0	3.5	0.0	0.0
150,001–200,000	24.5	17.9	2.9	17.0	0.0	2.8	0.0	19.6
Above 200,000	24.5	47.4	10.5	20.5	0.0	72.0	0.0	73.9
Total	100.0 (150)	100.0 (150)	100.0 (200)	100.0 (200)	100.0 (150)	100.0 (150)	0.0 (200)	100.0 (200)

Table 4.11 reveals that after rehabilitation households owned many household appliances, like radios, TVs, and vehicles. This indicates that after rehabilitation, households are better off and more comfortably living with all necessary facilities both for day-to-day communication and for doing household activities. Not only this, the value of household appliances as indicated by households is very high after the rehabilitation when compared to before rehabilitation both for rural and urban resettlers (table 4.12). Agricultural implements owned by households are presented in table 4.13. This indicates that most the households do not own any farm implements before and after rehabilitation.

Table 4.11 Percentage of Households That Own Household Appliances

	Urban		Rural		Total	
	Before Displacement	After Displacement	Before Displacement	After Displacement	Before Displacement	After Displacement
Radio/ TV	72.8	85.0	80.4	86.1	77.1	85.6
Vehicles	20.0	48.2	10.2	37.4	14.4	42.0
Others	5.2	7.9	7.4	8.5	6.5	8.2
Total sample	(150)	(150)	(200)	(200)	(350)	(350)

Solar panel at the residence of a sample household.

Table 4.12 Value of Household Appliances

(Rs.)

Value of household appliances	Urban (Percentage of Households)						Rural (Percentage of Households)					
	Before Displacement			After Displacement			Before Displacement			After Displacement		
	Radio/TV	Vehicles	Others	Radio/TV	Vehicles	Others	Radio/TV	Vehicles	Others	Radio/TV	Vehicles	Others
Up to 2,000	0.0	0.0	0.0	0.0	0.0	0.0	0.0	0.0	0.0	6.9	0.0	0.0
2,001–5,000	54.5	0.0	0.0	3.9	0.0	0.0	16.4	0.0	0.0	6.9	0.0	0.0
5,001–7,500	15.6	0.0	0.0	2.6	0.0	0.0	67.2	0.0	0.0	7.4	7.0	0.0
7,501–10,000	16.9	26.1	0.0	42.1	17.5	0.0	0.0	0.0	0.0	37.6	7.0	0.0
10,001–15,000	10.4	0.0	0.0	27.6	0.0	0.0	16.4	0.0	0.0	34.4	21.4	0.0
Above 15,000	2.6	73.9	100.0	23.7	82.5	100.0	0.0	0.0	0.0	6.9	38.0	0.0
Total sample HHs	(150)	(150)	(150)	(150)	(150)	(150)	(200)	(200)	(200)	(200)	(200)	(200)

Table 4.13 Agricultural Implements of Households (Percentage of Households That Own Implements)

	Urban		Rural		Total	
	Before Displacement	After Displacement	Before Displacement	After Displacement	Before Displacement	After Displacement
Tractor	3.3	5.0	2.0	7.8	2.6	6.6
Pumpset	0.0	0.0	2.0	34.0	1.1	19.4
Sprayer	0.0	0.0	7.0	12.0	4.0	6.9
Plough	0.0	0.0	50.0	85.0	28.6	48.6
Other agricultural implements	5.0	6.2	66.7	97.2	40.3	58.2
Sample HHs	(150)	(150)	(200)	(200)	(350)	(350)

Tractors usage at Raiwala.

PAFs also got adequately compensated for land, house, shops, trees, and assets based on market rates prevailing at the time of rehabilitation. Some PAFs have got compensation up to Rs. 1,000,000/- for land and for house construction (graph 4.7). On the same line, allowance/grant was given as incentive for timely shifting to resettlement areas, building construction allowance, decoration allowance, replacement allowance, food allowance, fertilizer allowance, and seed allowance. Among all allowances, constructing house was a major item both in rural and urban areas (graph 4.8).

Graph 4.7 Compensation Given to the Beneficiary

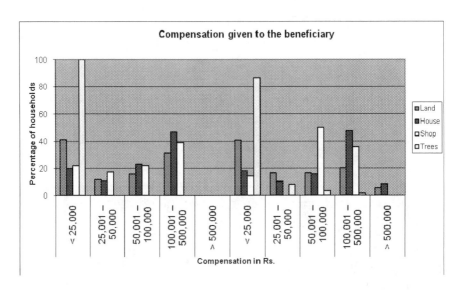

Graph 4.8 Allowances Given to the Beneficiary

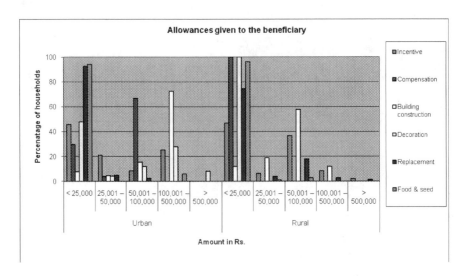

Chapter 5

Economic Aspects of Rehabilitation

From Landlessness to Land-Based Resettlement

Agricultural land is the primary source of income for the people living in the rural areas in India. However, to get higher earning and improved livelihood options, there should be sufficient land for cultivation along with supply of irrigation water and availability of other inputs like fertilizers, pesticides, seeds, etc. within the villages. Keeping this in mind, landless agricultural labourers of fully affected households in project-affected areas are also given the same benefits (i.e. 2 acres of land at free of cost at rural rehabilitation sites). Each displaced family, even if its acquired land is less than 2 acres, is given 2 acres of developed irrigated land, or half acre of developed irrigated land is offered adjacent to the municipal limits of Dehradun, Rishikesh, and Haridwar. If the cost of land acquired is more than the allotted land, the oustees will be paid the difference in cost, and if it is less, the difference in cost will not be recovered by THDC.

The previous chapter discussed about the social aspects of the households. In this chapter, the economic aspects of the PAPs were discussed. The number of rural habitants whose land was up to 0.5 acres and 1.1–2.5 acres has gone up after rehabilitation. Proportion of households who own up to 0.5-acre land and also households with 1.1 to 2.5 acres of land increased significantly after rehabilitation (graph 5.1) as most of the rural/urban households either got land of about 2.5 acres in rural areas or about 0.5 acres in semi-urban areas. Land value, as reported by households before and after rehabilitation, is presented in table 5.2. Most of the households could not disclose the actual land value. It was found out by the ASCI team that the value of land has gone up enormously after rehabilitation. It shows that the land value is significantly higher after rehabilitation even though many of them opted for only 0.5 acres of land. The land value of semi-urban areas is very high. During the survey, many households said that the market price of their land (0.5 acre) is more than 20 lakh. However, they are unable to make use of this land asset for economic activities as they are not able to use this land for agricultural activities due to limited land. Also, they are not able to sell the land to invest in other non-farm activities for which there is a lot of scope in these semi-urban areas. In the case of urban PAPs, households with 0.5 acres increased along with households with 2.5 acres of land as some of the urban inhabitants chose to resettle in semi-urban and rural areas.

Graph 5.1 Distribution of Household Land Holding

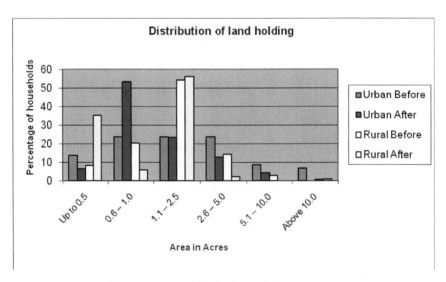

Note: 1 acre = 5 bigha/20 nali/100 sq. m

About 30% of the sample households own agricultural land up to one acre, and 47% of PAFs are having 1.0 to 2.5 acres of land before displacement (graph

5.1). The proportion has increased after the displacement was made by THDC. 45% of the sample households are having up to one-acre land, and 50% of the sample households are having 1 to 2.5 acres of agricultural land after displacement. The average size of land holding of the sample household has increased from 1.7 acres before displacement to 1.9 acres after displacement.

Table 5.2 Value of the Land of the Household

(Rs.)

value of land	Urban				Rural				Total			
	Before Displacement		After Displacement		Before Displacement		After Displacement		Before Displacement		After Displacement	
	Irrigated	Unirrigated	Irrigated	Unirrigated	Irrigated	Unirrigated	Irrigated	Unirrigated	Irrigated	Unirrigated	Irrigated	Unirrigated
Up to 25,000	50.0	0.0	25.0	0.0	10.0	0.0	0.0	0.0	14.7	0.0	3.7	0.0
25,001–50,000	0.0	0.0	0.0	0.0	16.7	0.0	0.0	0.0	14.7	0.0	0.0	0.0
50,001–75,000	0.0	0.0	0.0	0.0	10.0	0.0	0.0	0.0	8.8	0.0	0.0	0.0
75,001–100,000	0.0	0.0	25.0	0.0	6.7	0.0	4.3	0.0	5.9	0.0	7.4	0.0
100,001–150,000	0.0	0.0	25.0	0.0	6.7	0.0	13.0	0.0	5.9	0.0	14.8	0.0
Above 150,000	50.0	0.0	25.0	0.0	50.0	0.0	82.6	0.0	50.0	0.0	74.1	0.0
All	100 (150)	100 (150)	100 (150)	100 (150)	100 (200)	100 (200)	100 (200)	100 (200)	100 (350)	100 (350)	100 (350)	100 (350)

As a result of land development and creation of irrigation facilities, households with tube well irrigation facilities have increased significantly from 61% of rural households before rehabilitation to 98% households after rehabilitation (table 5.3). Tube well is the major source of irrigation before and after rehabilitation. As against depending only on the government for the source of irrigation, now a few households made their own arrangements for their irrigation sources, like electric pumpset and diesel pumpset.

Table 5.3 Details about Irrigation in Rural Areas

type of irrigation	Before Displacement			After Displacement		
	Own	Government	Total	Own	Government	Total
Gravity irrigation	0.0	5.2	5.2	0.0	4.6	4.6
Electrical pumpset	0.0	2.6	2.6	25.0	2.6	27.6
Diesel pumpset	0.0	1.9	1.9	25.0	2.0	27.0
Tank/canal	0.0	29.2	29.2	25.0	18.3	43.3
Tube well	0.0	61.0	61.0	25.0	72.5	97.5

The irrigation facilities have also improved significantly after the displacement because the THDC has developed/constructed irrigation canals/channels to most of the agricultural lands provided to the PAPs. Such type of system was not available in the previous location. As a result, farmers are growing three crops in a year. Kharif paddy is the main crop even though most of the farmers also grow sugar cane. Most of the farmers in suburban areas grow vegetable crops, like tomato, cabbage, cauliflower, brinjal, and potato.

Livestock, like buffaloes, bulls, and cows, is one of the main assets of households before rehabilitation. The livestock has come down after rehabilitation (table 5.4). Before rehabilitation, the households used to make use of the livestock for both agricultural purpose and nutrition (milk). Moreover, there was no difficulty in feeding the livestock before rehabilitation as plenty of grass was available in the hillocks. After rehabilitation, the household livestock decreased due to feed and limited availability of land for grazing purpose.

Table 5.4 Number of Livestock Owned by Sample Households

	Urban		Rural		Total	
	Before Displacement	After Displacement	Before Displacement	After Displacement	Before Displacement	After Displacement
Buffalos	4	1	170	79	174	80
Bulls	4	0	125	3	129	3
Cows	18	4	93	27	111	31
Goats/sheep	10	0	30	4	40	4

From Joblessness to Reemployment

Distribution of households according to main occupation is given in table 5.5. Overall households engaged in family business increased from 24% before displacement to 31% after displacement, while persons engaged in government services increased from 9.7% before rehabilitation to 11.4% after rehabilitation. Traditionally, these two categories are high-income earning and high-social-status occupations, which indicates that overall there is an increase in employment opportunities after rehabilitation. In rural areas, there is no change in the households whose occupation is agriculture. After rehabilitation, the number of households who engaged themselves in family business, government service, and other employment has increased because of their proximity to urban areas. In urban areas, those who engaged in family business increased by 12.7% compared to before rehabilitation. Interestingly, housewives after rehabilitation got engaged in some economic activity and earning incomes. This is a significant development in the urban areas.

Fish business at New Tehri Town.

In rural areas, about 36% of rehabilitated population depend on agriculture. Families dependent on agriculture are stagnant. Households dependent on family business increased from 12% to 16%. Government servants increased from 11% to 16%. In urban areas, family business increased from 53% to 60%. Most of the women also participated in household business, and women participation rate in overall employment increased significantly in urban areas.

Table 5.5 Distribution of Main Occupation of the Households before and after Displacement

main occupation	Urban		Rural		Total	
	Before Displacement	After Displacement	Before Displacement	After Displacement	Before Displacement	After Displacement
Agriculture	2.7	0.0	36.8	36.0	22.2	20.6
Agricultural labourer	3.5	1.5	1.1	1.0	2.1	1.2
Family business	53.1	59.8	12.6	15.5	30.0	34.5
Government service	10.6	6.8	11.6	15.5	11.2	11.8
Transport	0.0	1.5	4.2	2.0	2.4	1.8
Retired employee	5.3	7.6	10.0	6.5	8.0	7.0
Employee	19.5	15.9	18.9	20.5	19.2	18.5
THDC employee	1.8	1.5	1.6	1.0	1.7	1.2
Others	3.5	5.3	3.2	2.0	3.3	3.4
Total	100.0 (150)	100.0 (150)	100.0 (200)	100.0 (200)	100.0 (350)	100.0 (350)

Table 5.6 Distribution of Days of Employment of Households in a Year

days of employment	Urban		Rural		Total	
	Before Displacement	After Displacement	Before Displacement	After Displacement	Before Displacement	After Displacement
Up to 50	0.0	0.0	1.8	0.0	0.7	0.0
51–100	0.0	0.0	1.8	0.0	0.7	0.0
101–150	0.0	0.0	0.0	0.0	0.0	0.0
151–200	3.4	0.0	10.7	5.6	6.2	5.0
201–250	3.4	0.0	3.6	0.0	3.4	0.0
251–300	1.1	0.0	1.8	0.0	1.4	0.0
Above 300	92.1	100.0	80.4	94.4	87.6	95.0
Total	100.0 (150)	100.0 (150)	100.0 (200)	100.0 (200)	100.0 (350)	100.0 (350)

The number of days of employment increased significantly after rehabilitation. Persons who worked for more than 300 days per annum increased from 88% before rehabilitation to 95% after rehabilitation (table 5.6). THDC has given jobs to workmen and supervisors and ordered the contractors of the THDC to recruit unskilled workers, clerical staff, and supervisors. THDC awarded small-sized contracts for some of the PAPs and gave special preference in local developmental works. The state government also initiated various self-employment/income-generating schemes for the benefit of PAPs, like poultry-farming, floriculture, pisciculture, animal husbandry, handicrafts, and khadi work.

The number of days of employment increased significantly due to the rehabilitation benefits provided by the THDC. The opportunities for rural PAPs have been increased because they have allotted agricultural land with irrigation facility which helps in cultivating short-duration high-yielding varieties of crops, like vegetables, paddy, wheat, pulses, and oilseeds. They also started growing commercial crops, like fruits, sugar cane, potato, and sweetcorn, by using modern farming equipments. The PAPs rehabilitated close to urban areas are benefited by the construction and opening of shops at their allotted land, cultivating vegetables, fruits, sweetcorn, etc. in their half-acre land which was allotted by THDC. In addition to that, they had a chance to get work in industries, service, transport, and other sectors available in cities only.

Paddy field at Banjarawala.

Income distribution of households in urban areas (table 5.7) shows that there is a marginal increase in the number of household income from government employment while income from dairy and goat-rearing/sheep-rearing has reduced significantly. Income from cottage industries is stagnant, while income from other trade and construction-related activities, like electrician and plumber, has increased. Overall participatory appraisal showed that there was less scope for traditional employment in the resettled sites. On the other hand, there is greater scope and emerging need for skill-based employment for youth in resettled sites, which needs to be exploited with proper training for youth, including women, and market-support arrangements by the government.

Table 5.7 Income Distribution of Households in Urban Households

(Rs./year/HH)

occupation	Before Displacement							After Displacement						
	Up to 5,000	5,001–7,500	7,501–10,000	10,001–15,000	15,001–20,000	20,001–25,000	Above 25,000	Up to 5,000	5,001–7,500	7,501–10,000	10,001–15,000	15,001–20,000	20,001–25,000	Above 25,000
Dairy	1.7	11.1	7.7	0.0	0.0	0.0	0.0	0.0	0.0	6.3	0.0	0.0	0.0	0.0
Goat-rearing/sheep-rearing	1.7	0.0	0.0	8.3	0.0	0.0	0.0	0.0	7.1	6.3	0.0	0.0	0.0	0.0
Non-agricultural employment	5.0	0.0	0.0	0.0	0.0	0.0	0.0	12.3	0.0	0.0	0.0	6.7	0.0	0.0
Skilled worker	6.7	0.0	0.0	0.0	0.0	0.0	0.0	4.6	7.1	0.0	10.0	0.0	0.0	0.0
Government employment	31.7	66.7	30.8	58.3	0.0	100.0	10.7	23.1	64.3	37.5	40.0	26.7	0.0	16.7
Cottage industry/self-employment (shop, etc.)	26.7	11.1	15.4	25.0	25.0	0.0	7.1	26.2	0.0	6.3	10.0	13.3	0.0	0.0
Other trades (electrician, plumber, etc.)	26.7	11.1	46.2	8.3	75.0	0.0	82.1	33.8	21.4	43.8	40.0	53.3	100.0	83.3
All	100 (80)	100 (17)	100 (17)	100 (11)	100 (5)	100 (1)	100 (19)	100 (50)	100 (12)	100 (15)	100 (14)	100 (16)	100 (10)	100 (33)

Income distribution of households in rural areas (table 5.8) shows that income from agriculture increased significantly, while income from agricultural labourer and dairy has remained stagnant. Many of the rural agricultural households moved from lower income brackets before rehabilitation to higher income brackets after rehabilitation. This was mainly due to assured irrigation and proximity to urban/semi-urban areas to market their produce. Income from non-agricultural employment increased marginally. While household industries and cottage industries were stagnant, income from other trade and construction-related activities, like electrical work and plumbing has increased marginally as in the case of urban households. Overall participatory appraisal showed that there was good scope for increasing agricultural productivity in the resettled areas as the soils are fertile and there is no shortage of irrigation water throughout the year. However, about 44% of PAFs in both urban and rural areas are of the opinion that the new place has opportunities for income and other employment opportunities. Most of the PAFs who opted for 0.5 acres in suburban areas and are living in NTT are in need of increasing employment opportunities, especially for educated youth. In urban areas, there has been no change to those who were in government employment, but some of them have moved to higher income bracket over a period of time. But there has been a significant change in households who are in other trades such as electrician and plumber. Here also many of them have moved to higher income brackets. This shows that there are opportunities for income and employment in the new place.

Shop in Pathri.

Table 5.8 Income Distribution of Households in Rural Households

(Rs./year/HH)

occupation	Before Displacement							After Displacement						
	Up to 5,000	5,001–7,500	7,501–10,000	10,001–15,000	15,001–20,000	20,001–25,000	Above 25,000	Up to 5,000	5,001–7,500	7,501–10,000	10,001–15,000	15,001–20,000	20,001–25,000	Above 25,000
Agriculture	34.9	0.0	41.2	57.1	87.5	75.0	93.3	32.1	33.3	71.8	73.9	46.2	100.0	73.1
Agricultural labour	1.6	0.0	5.9	0.0	0.0	0.0	0.0	1.8	0.0	0.0	4.3	7.7	0.0	0.0
Dairy	3.1	0.0	5.9	0.0	0.0	0.0	0.0	3.0	0.0	0.0	0.0	0.0	0.0	0.0
Goat-rearing/sheep-rearing	20.3	0.0	5.9	0.0	0.0	0.0	0.0	11.9	0.0	2.6	0.0	0.0	0.0	0.0
Non-agricultural employment	6.8	50.0	0.0	0.0	0.0	0.0	0.0	10.7	0.0	2.6	0.0	0.0	0.0	3.8
Household industry/business	12.0	0.0	0.0	0.0	0.0	0.0	0.0	11.3	0.0	0.0	0.0	0.0	0.0	0.0
Skilled worker (electrician, plumber, etc.)	1.0	0.0	0.0	0.0	0.0	0.0	0.0	1.2	8.3	0.0	0.0	0.0	0.0	3.8
Government employment	12.0	50.0	29.4	28.6	12.5	25.0	1.7	10.7	41.7	20.5	13.0	30.8	0.0	11.5
Others	8.3	0.0	11.8	14.3	0.0	0.0	5.0	17.3	16.7	2.6	8.7	15.4	0.0	7.7
All	100 (132)	100 (20)	100 (21)	100 (5)	100 (4)	100 (5)	100 (13)	100 (117)	100 (8)	100 (27)	100 (16)	100 (9)	100 (5)	100 (18)

Vegetable cultivation in Banjarawala.

The expenditure of households in urban and rural areas is given in tables 5.9 and 5.10 respectively. Most of the households were spending up to Rs. 5,000 on food, education, clothing, and health before displacement. The same trend continues after rehabilitation as well. There is a decrease in the number of households whose expenditure was up to Rs. 5,000, and at the same time, the number of households whose income is above Rs. 5,000 has increased. In rural areas, the number of households whose expenditure was more than Rs. 5,000 has increased after rehabilitation. It shows that the households were affording to spend more than Rs. 5,000 because of higher incomes after rehabilitation. In rural areas, households were able to spend more on education, clothing, and transport, which is a positive development. Now many of the households have their own transport which was not the case before rehabilitation in rural areas (table 5.9). On the whole, with the increase in incomes after rehabilitation, they could spend more on their food, clothing, education, and transport.

Table 5.9 Expenditure of the Households in Urban Areas

(Rs./year/HH)

item	Before Displacement							After Displacement						
	Up to 5,000	5,001–7,500	7,501–10,000	10,001–15,000	15,001–20,000	20,001–25,000	Above 25,000	Up to 5,000	5,001–7,500	7,501–10,000	10,001–15,000	15,001–20,000	20,001–25,000	Above 25,000
Food	22.4	30	27	28.6	31	24	21	19.6	73.3	85.7	37.5	0.0	0.0	25.0
Housing	4	4	5	24	3	7	8	0.0	0.0	0.0	0.0	0.0	0.0	0.0
Education	20.9	27	12	20	10	13	12	18.3	26.7	14.3	0.0	0.0	0.0	75.0
Clothing	20	15	12	14	21	10	13	24.2	0.0	0.0	12.5	50.0	0.0	0.0
Health	17.7	4	7	3	13	10	12	17.1	0.0	0.0	0.0	50.0	0.0	0.0
Vehicles/transport	7.5	6	18	6	13	15	16	10.5	0.0	0.0	25.0	0.0	0.0	0.0
Entertainment	6.7	14.3	14	4	7	10	10	10.3	0.0	0.0	25.0	0.0	0.0	0.0
Others	0	0	5	0	2	10	8	0.0	0.0	0.0	0.0	0.0	0.0	0.0
All	100 (115)	100 (17)	100 (10)	100 (2)	100 (2)	100 (3)	100 (1)	100 (90)	100 (8)	100 (7)	100 (10)	100 (7)	100 (13)	100 (15)

Table 5.10 Expenditure of the Households in Rural Areas

(Rs./year/HH)

item	Before Displacement							After Displacement						
	Up to 5,000	5,001–7,500	7,501–10,000	10,001–15,000	15,001–20,000	20,001–25,000	Above 25,000	Up to 5,000	5,001–7,500	7,501–10,000	10,001–15,000	15,001–20,000	20,001–25,000	Above 25,000
Food	23.3	28	27	23	19	16	23.3	24	30	27	16	27	15	21
Housing	5	8	9	3	7	4	7	8	4	5	4	4	7	10
Education	25.7	21	20	24	23	21	18	17	27	12	21	18	24	13
Clothing	28	21	25	21	25	23	20	15	15	12	23	20	18	18
Health	15	7	12	7	12	17	20	12	4	7	17	10	10	12
Vehicles/transport	2	8	2	9	10	9	10	10	6	18	9	10	9	6
Entertainment	1	7	5	13	4	10	1.5	1.5	14.3	14	10	1.5	10	7
Others	0	0	0	0	0	0	0	12	0	5	0	9	7	13
All	100 (174)	100 (12)	100 (3)	100 (5)	100 (3)	100 (2)	100 (1)	100 (152)	100 (14)	100 (6)	100 (7)	100 (5)	100 (11)	100 (5)

Petrol-filling station in New Tehri Town.

Office in New Tehri Town.

Chapter 6

Community Aspects
of Rehabilitation

From Marginalization to Social Inclusion

This chapter explains the community-related aspects of rehabilitation. As mentioned earlier, THDC has provided amenities for the community at the rehabilitation sites. The community and also the households were asked about these facilities and their usefulness. Below, the responses of households were discussed.

Women Empowerment

Almost all the respondents in the rural and urban sample households expressed that there was no discrimination, no violence, and no restrictions imposed on women (graphs 6.1, 6.2, 6.3). About 90–98% of the respondents have expressed these opinions. Generally, they participate in social and economic activities at their newly developed rehabilitated colonies/locations, and they also mingle with host population freely.

Graph 6.1 Whether Any Discrimination Shown towards Women at New Localities

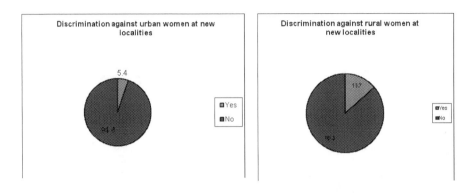

Discrimination against urban women at new localities

5.4

94.6

☒Yes
☒No

Discrimination against rural women at new localities

13.7

86.3

☒Yes
☒No

Clinic for females in Pathri.

Graph 6.2 Whether Any Violence against Women at New Localities

Graph 6.3 Whether Women Have Any Restrictions in New Localities

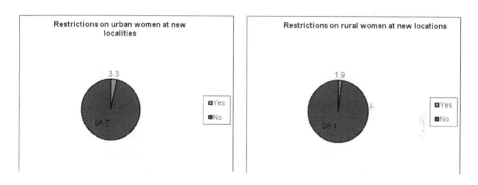

The socio-economic profile of the women in both rural and urban areas after displacement in terms of status in the village and at home has increased significantly. Even though source of income and employment in traditional activities decreased marginally for women, other employment opportunities and educational facilities for women increased significantly in both the urban and rural PAPs (graph 6.4).

Graph 6.4 Changes in the Socio-Economic Profile of the Women after Displacement

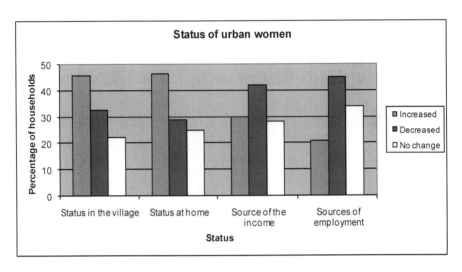

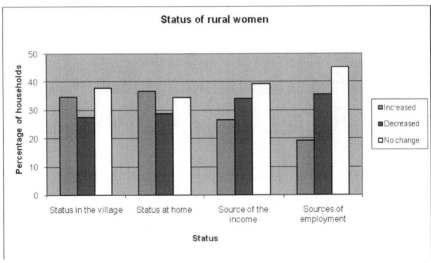

Children playing at school in Raiwala

From Loss of Access to Restoration of Community Assets and Services

A. Primary Education

Among the urban sample households, three-fourths of them were residing less than 1 km distance from the primary school before rehabilitation. The proportion has come down to half after rehabilitation (table 6.5). This was because in Old Tehri Town, being a compact area, all the facilities were available within the area. In New Tehri Town, being a bigger area, the facilities were scattered a little more. Among the rural sample households, half were residing less than 1 km from the primary school before and after rehabilitation (table 6.6).

About half of the sample households were satisfied with the primary education facilities available in urban areas, and around one-fourth were satisfied with the rural areas after rehabilitation (table 6.7). 15% of them are more satisfied, 40% are moderately satisfied, and 45% are not satisfied among urban sample households, whereas 21% are more satisfied, 48% are moderately satisfied, and 31% are not satisfied among rural sample households. A significant number of them expressed that they are not satisfied with the facilities. This was due to very high expectations of households from THDC. Most of these facilities, particularly in rural areas, were not at all available before rehabilitation.

The quality of education in terms of infrastructure (e.g. building, playground) and other facilities like sanitation, drinking water, ventilation, furniture, etc. has improved a lot in the newly constructed rehabilitated colonies. The accessibility to the school from their houses is also made easy with the road network developed by the THDC, which was absent in the previous locations.

B. Middle School Education

Among the urban sample households, three-fourths were residing less than 1 km from the middle school before rehabilitation, whereas the proportion has come down to three-fifths after rehabilitation (table 6.5). Among the rural sample households, around 30% were residing in less than 1 km distance from the middle school before and after rehabilitation (table 6.6).

About half of the urban resettlers and about one-fourth of the rural resettlers are satisfied with the middle school education facilities available in the rehabilitation sites (table 6.7). Among urban resettlers, 23% are highly satisfied, 28% are moderately satisfied, and 48% are not satisfied. In rural areas, about 22% are highly satisfied, 48% are moderately satisfied, and 30% are not satisfied with the middle school education facilities available at rehabilitation sites.

View of New Tehri Town

Table 6.5 Distance from the Residence to Various Important Locations of the Urban Community

(km)

facility	Before Displacement						After Displacement					
	≤0.1	1.1–3.0	3.1–5.0	5.1–10.0	>10.0	All	≤0.1	1.1–3.0	3.1–5.0	5.1–10.0	>10.0	All
Hospital	70	21.3	1.3	5	2.5	100	47.7	34.1	11.4	2.3	4.5	100
Primary education	75	17.5	2.5	3.8	1.3	100	53	33.7	8.4	3.6	1.2	100
Middle school education	72.2	21.5	1.3	2.5	2.5	100	58.4	28.6	7.8	5.2	0	100
Drinking water	87.1	9.7	0	0	3.2	100	72.7	21.2	6.1	0	0	100
Market	78	15.3	0	5.1	1.7	100	66.2	28.2	4.2	1.4	0	100
Road connectivity	90.3	6.5	1.6	0	1.6	100	77.8	15.9	4.8	0	1.6	100
Inner road	93.4	3.3	0	0	3.3	100	81	10.3	5.2	0	3.4	100
Workplace	87.5	9.4	0	0	3.1	100	61.8	17.6	5.9	5.9	8.8	100
Post office	66.7	23.6	1.4	2.8	5.6	100	44.2	42.9	11.7	0	1.3	100
Bank/microfinance	70.4	21.1	2.8	1.4	4.2	100	58.9	26	11	1.4	2.7	100
Neighbouring shop	85.9	12.5	0	0	1.6	100	68.9	24.6	4.9	0	1.6	100
Shop for agricultural inputs	84.8	12.1	0	1.5	1.5	100	73.8	20	4.6	0	1.5	100
PDS/ration shop	83.6	11.5	1.6	1.6	1.6	100	77.8	15.9	4.8	1.6	1.6	100
PCO	85.5	10.9	0	1.8	1.8	100	72.5	15.7	9.8	0	2	100

Table 6.6 Distance from the Residence to Various Important Locations of the Rural Community

(km)

facility	Before Displacement						After Displacement					
	≤0.1	1.1–3.0	3.1–5.0	5.1–10.0	>10.0	All	≤0.1	1.1–3.0	3.1–5.0	5.1–10.0	>10.0	All
Hospital	12.3	15.5	26.2	39.6	6.4	100	4.2	16.8	17.4	26.8	34.7	100
Primary education	48.3	30.5	17.2	4	0	100	49.7	34.7	9.6	4.8	1.2	100
Middle school education	31	39.9	21.5	5.7	1.9	100	29	34.8	18.7	11	6.5	100
Drinking water	74	16.4	4.1	5.5	0	100	76.2	7.9	4.8	4.8	6.3	100
Market	21.6	26.8	25.5	20.9	5.2	100	17.7	19.5	26.2	15.2	21.3	100
Road connectivity	49.6	33.6	10.7	4.6	1.5	100	56.4	25.7	10	2.9	5	100
Inner road	79.2	15.1	0.9	4.7	0	100	81.2	11.9	3	3	1	100
Workplace	51.7	33.3	3.3	3.3	8.3	100	67.2	14.8	4.9	6.6	6.6	100
Post office	30.4	37.3	24.2	6.8	1.2	100	14.9	44.7	23.6	12.4	4.3	100
Bank/microfinance	21.4	38.4	22	15.1	3.1	100	17.9	35.9	26.3	12.2	7.7	100
Neighbouring shop	70.9	23.9	4.3	0.9	0	100	67.3	25.7	4.4	1.8	0.9	100
Shop for agricultural inputs	47.5	37.6	10.9	3	1	100	44.9	41.6	3.4	1.1	9	100
PDS/ration shop	51.5	34	11.3	2.1	1	100	58.1	32.3	6.5	2.2	1.1	100
PCO	58.7	28.6	9.5	3.2	0	100	66.1	27.4	4.8	1.6	0	100

Shopping complex at New Tehri Town.

Table 6.7 Satisfactory Levels on Basic Needs of the Community after Rehabilitation

	Urban				Rural			
	More Satisfied	Moderately Satisfied	Not Satisfied	All	More Satisfied	Moderately Satisfied	Not Satisfied	All
Hospital	10.1	37.7	52.2	100	10.8	45.1	44.1	100
Primary education	14.9	40.3	44.8	100	21.2	47.5	31.3	100
Middle school education	23.4	28.1	48.4	100	21.9	47.9	30.2	100
Drinking water	21.5	30.8	47.7	100	24.4	50	25.6	100
Market	19.7	40.9	39.4	100	18.3	53.8	28	100
Road connectivity	22.8	45.6	31.6	100	11.6	53.5	34.9	100
Inner road	24.5	43.4	32.1	100	15.9	51.2	32.9	100
Workplace	23.3	41.9	34.9	100	15.5	49.3	35.2	100
Sanitation	17.5	50	32.5	100	17.9	43.3	38.8	100
Electricity	20.4	46.3	33.3	100	23.5	51.9	24.7	100
Irrigation	10.5	52.6	36.8	100	13.9	51.9	34.2	100
Post office	19.6	44.6	35.7	100	13.2	54.9	31.9	100
Bank/microfinance	19	52.4	28.6	100	14.4	54.4	31.1	100
Neighbouring shop	17.7	51.6	30.6	100	24.4	54.9	20.7	100
Shop for agricultural inputs	16.4	54.1	29.5	100	17.9	52.6	29.5	100
PDS/ration shop	16.4	55.7	27.9	100	25.7	47.1	27.1	100
PCO	16.4	59	24.6	100	27.4	46.8	25.8	100

Head post office at New Tehri Town.

The facilities like religious place, park, panchayat office, function hall which were not available before rehabilitation have been provided by THDC. Other facilities like village pond and pastured land were not available in some places as these were beyond the purview of THDC.

Dormitory in Pashulok.

Table 6.8 Community Meetings/Common Facilities in the Rehabilitation Place

Facility	Urban			Rural		
	Available	Not Available	All	Available	Not Available	All
Religious place	82.5	17.5	100	79.4	20.6	100
Park	48.9	51.1	100	44	56	100
Panchayat office	52.4	47.6	100	49	51	100
Function hall	33.1	66.9	100	32.4	67.6	100
Graveyard	17.4	82.6	100	15.2	84.8	100
Entertainment/cinema	8	92	100	10.3	89.7	100
Shared common property	8.9	91.1	100	5.6	94.4	100
Village pond	8	92	100	5.3	94.7	100
Forest resources	24	76	100	5.4	94.6	100
Fuel	21.1	78.9	100	8.4	91.6	100
Pastured land	7.8	92.2	100	5.3	94.7	100

When enquired about the suggestions/comments, the households expressed a host of facilities to be provided by the THDC. Already, THDC provided facilities like drinking water, education facilities, electricity, function halls, hospital, etc. The households need a lot more facilities provided by the THDC (table 6.9) which are beyond the scope of THDC's rehabilitation policy.

Table 6.9 Suggestions/Comments Made by the Respondents

(Percentage of population within urban/rural areas)

	Urban Respondents	Rural Respondents
Drinking-water facilities to be improved	37.3	30.5
Public transport to be strengthened	17.3	28.5
Employment opportunities declined to be improved	27.3	26.0
Hospital/medical facilities being far away	11.3	25.5
Metalled inner roads to be repaired	7.3	20.0
Drainage facilities to be improved in flood affected areas	5.3	18.0
Education facilities to be improved	8.7	17.5
Irrigation water to be available for all seasons	0.0	16.5
Compensation low or yet to be received	24.0	14.0
Electricity to be uninterrupted	11.3	11.0
Parks for children not maintained	4.0	11.0
Sanitation facilities to be improved	3.3	9.0
Bank facilities to be improved	2.0	6.0
Post office being far away	3.3	6.0
Supply of gas for domestic purpose	0.0	4.5
Street lights in interior places	0.0	4.5
Function hall being far away	2.7	4.0
Recreation facilities like cinema halls being far away	2.0	3.0
Ration shop being far away	0.0	2.5
Veterinary hospital to be established	0.0	2.0
Business declined in current location	14.7	0.0
Other miscellaneous problems	28.0	42.5

Electricity

From table 6.7, it was observed that about two-thirds of the urban sample households and three-fourths of the rural sample households were satisfied with the electricity facilities and uninterrupted power supply. On an average, the number of hours of power supply has increased from 13 hours a day to 18 hours a day. Among urban households, 21% are highly satisfied, 46% are moderately satisfied, and 33% are not satisfied, whereas among rural households, 23% are highly satisfied, 52% are moderately satisfied, and 25% are not satisfied.

New Tehri Town at night.

Sanitation

About two-third of the urban sample households and three-fifth of the rural sample households were satisfied with the sanitation facilities in the resettlement locations (table 6.7). Among urban households, 18% were highly satisfied, 50% were moderately satisfied, and 32% were not satisfied. In rural households, 18% were highly satisfied, 43% were moderately satisfied, and 39% were not satisfied.

Irrigation

About two-thirds of rural sample households were satisfied with the irrigation facilities (both main canal and internal channels) provided for their agriculture lands by the THDC (table 6.7). Among rural households, 14% are highly satisfied, 52% are moderately satisfied, and 34% are not satisfied.

Post Office

About 90% of the urban households have the access to post office within a radius of 3 km before and after displacement (table 6.5). The distance is more in the rural resettlement sites. About two-thirds of PAPs have the access to post office within 3 km before rehabilitation, whereas 60% have access after rehabilitation (table 6.6).

About two-third of the urban and rural sample households were satisfied with access to the post office facilities (table 6.7). Among urban households, 20% are highly satisfied, 45% are moderately satisfied, and 35% are not satisfied. Among rural households, 13% are highly satisfied, 55% are moderately satisfied, and 32% are not satisfied.

Health

The distance to hospital from house is below 1 km for about 70% of the sample households and below 3 km for about 21% of the households for urban resettlers before rehabilitation. After rehabilitation, the distance between house and hospital is below 1 km for about 48% of the resettlers, up to 3 km for about 34% of the resettlers, and above 3 km radius for 18% of the households in urban sites after rehabilitation (table 6.5). The distance between house and hospital is below 3 km for about 28% of the households, below 10 km for about 66% of the residents in rural areas before rehabilitation, whereas about 21% of the sample households reside below 3 km distance from the nearest hospital and about 79% reside more than 3 km radius in rural areas after rehabilitation. However, due to improved transport facilities and good roads, most of the resettlers feel that the time consumed in travelling between house and hospital has been reduced significantly.

About half of the sample households were satisfied with the medical facilities available in both urban and rural areas (table 6.7). 10% are highly satisfied, 38% are moderately satisfied, and 52% are not satisfied among urban PAPs, whereas 11% are highly satisfied, 45% are moderately satisfied, and 44% are not satisfied among rural sample households. In the rehabilitated locations developed by the THDC, quality medical care is made available because the THDC has constructed the necessary hospitals/primary health centres (PHCs) at their rehabilitated colonies only. Previously, they had to visit nearby city to get qualified medical care as at that time qualified medical doctors were not located within villages.

Government hospital in New Tehri Town.

Roads

The network of inner roads as well as the main roads is well laid and maintained in both the urban and rural rehabilitated colonies when compared with the previous settlements. Two-thirds of the urban and rural PAFs are satisfied with the roads laid by the THDC. 24% of PAFs are highly satisfied, 44% are moderately satisfied, and 32% are not satisfied among urban resettlers, whereas 14% are highly satisfied, 52% are moderately satisfied, and 34% are not satisfied among rural PAFs.

Blacktop road in New Tehri Town.

Drinking Water

Most of the sample households, both in rural and urban colonies, were provided with safe drinking water within a radius of 1 km during before and after replacement. About half of the urban rehabilitated sample and three-fourths of the rural rehabilitated sample households are satisfied with the safe drinking-water facility provided by the THDC (table 6.7). About 21% are highly satisfied, 31% are moderately satisfied, and 48% are not satisfied among urban households, whereas 24% are highly satisfied and 50% are moderately satisfied among rural households.

Drinking water tank in Raiwala.

Market

Among the urban PAFs, three-fourths were residing in less than 1 km distance from the market before rehabilitation, whereas the proportion has come down to two-thirds after rehabilitation (table 6.5). However, many respondents informed us that after rehabilitation, improvement in transport facilities has reduced travel time to reach markets. Among the rural sample, one-fifth of the total households were residing within 1 km from the market after rehabilitation (table 6.6). Around three-fifths of the PAFs were satisfied with the market facilities available in urban areas, and about three-fourths were satisfied in the rural areas (table 6.7). About 20% were highly satisfied, and 41% are moderately satisfied among urban PAFs, whereas 18% are highly satisfied, and 54% are moderately satisfied among rural PAFs.

Shopping complex in New Tehri Town.

Workplace

Among the urban PAFs, about 88% were residing within 1 km distance from the workplace before rehabilitation, whereas the proportion has come down to two-thirds after rehabilitation. Among the rural sample households, half of the total PAFs were residing within 1 km from the workplace before rehabilitation, whereas the proportion has gone up to two-thirds after rehabilitation. These figures indicates that, especially in the rural areas, the distance for market, workplace, and other economic activity centres has come down after rehabilitation in addition to the better roads and transport facilities.

Around two-thirds of the sample households were satisfied with the workplace in both urban and rural areas. 23% are highly satisfied, 42% are moderately satisfied, and 35% are not satisfied among urban sample households, whereas 15% are highly satisfied, 49% are moderately satisfied, and 35% are not satisfied among rural sample households.

Bank/Microfinance Institution

Among the urban sample households, around 70% were residing less than 1 km from the bank/microfinance institution before rehabilitation, whereas the proportion has come down to 60% after rehabilitation. Among the rural sample households, about 20% of the PAPs were residing less than 1 km from the bank/microfinance institution before and after rehabilitation.

Around two-thirds of the sample households were satisfied with the availability of credit and facilities provided by banks/microfinance institutions in both urban and rural areas. 19% are highly satisfied, and 52% are moderately satisfied among urban sample households, whereas 14% are highly satisfied, and 55% are moderately satisfied among rural sample households.

Bank in New Tehri Town.

Neighbouring Shop

Among the urban sample households, around 86% were residing within 1 km from their neighbourhood shop before rehabilitation, whereas the proportion has come down to 69% after rehabilitation. Among the rural sample households, about 70% of the PAFs were residing less than 1 km from their neighbourhood shop before and after rehabilitation.

Around two-thirds of the sample households were satisfied with the neighbourhood shop in both urban and rural areas after rehabilitation. 18% were highly satisfied, and 52% are moderately satisfied among urban sample households, whereas 24% were highly satisfied, and 55% are moderately satisfied among rural sample households.

PDS/Ration Shop

Among the urban sample households, about four-fifths were residing within 1 km from the PDS/ration shop before and after rehabilitation. Among the rural sample, half of the PAFs were residing within 1 km from the PDS/ration shop before and after rehabilitation.

About three-fourths of the sample households were satisfied with the PDS/ration shop in both urban and rural areas. About 16% were highly satisfied, and 56% were moderately satisfied among urban sample households, whereas about 26% were more satisfied, and 47% are moderately satisfied among rural sample households.

PCO

Among the urban sample households, about 86% were residing within 1 km from the PCO before rehabilitation, whereas the proportion has come down to 73% after rehabilitation (table 6.5). Among the rural sample households, 59% of the total were residing less than 1 km from the PCO before rehabilitation, whereas the proportion has gone up to 66% after rehabilitation (table 6.6).

Around three-fourths of the sample households were satisfied with the PCO in both the urban and rural areas (table 6.7). About 16% were highly satisfied, and 59% were moderately satisfied among urban sample households, whereas about 27% were highly satisfied, and 47% were moderately satisfied among rural sample households.

Communication facilities in Banjarawala.

Common Facilities

About 83% urban sample households informed that the THDC has constructed religious places like temples, mosques, and gurdwaras in the colonies, whereas in rural sample households, 79% were satisfied with the religious places constructed in the rehabilitated colonies (table 6.7). However, the study team is of the opinion that large sums have been spent on religious places for construction of huge structures which were not utilized by the residents' respective religious groups.

Communications tower in New Tehri Town.

One of the important factors in successful implementation of R & R policy is the cooperation in rehabilitation and resettlement by the PAFs with the government. However, in the survey, most of the PAFs were not aware of the components of the project and its benefits both to the agricultural sector and drinking water and its potential to energy generation for both the rural and urban areas. Hence, it is important to sensitize the PAFs to the benefits of the project to the country at macro level and the compensation they get in return through awareness programmes. As expected, most of the PAFs do not like the new place when compared to the previous place. Only 36% of rehabilitated PAFs in urban settlements and about 50% of PAFs in rural settlements reported that they like the new resettlement sites compared to their earlier place of living and were satisfied with the facilities available at the new places (graph 6.6). General problems faced at rehabilitated sites and suggestions for the problems have been given in table 6.9. The common problems faced in urban resettlement areas are scarcity of drinking water, unemployment, lack of business and market opportunities and connections to other places, and lack of transport facilities.

While common problems faced in rural rehabilitated sites are scarcity of drinking water, lack of transport facilities, unemployment, inadequate medical facilities, lack of educational institutions, lack of all-weather road connectivity, lack of drainage facilities in some areas, and movement of wild animals. However, the intensity of these problems is not severe and can be corrected easily by the involvement of local governance institutions.

Graph 6.5 Whether the Households Liked the New Place

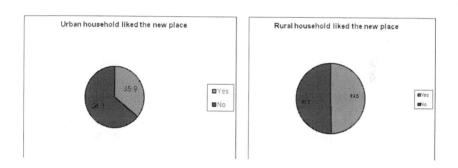

Graph 6.6 Whether the Households Are Satisfied with the Available Facilities

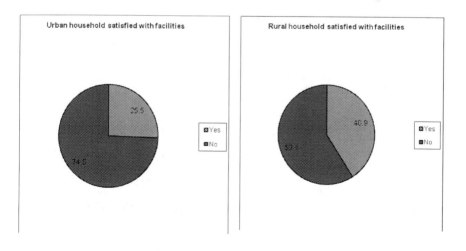

From Social Disarticulation to Networks and Community Rebuilding

In most of the urban and rural rehabilitated sites, most of the PAFs reported no disputes with the local population (graph 6.7). Further, there is a feeling of increasing cooperation among resettled population and previous habitants in most of the locations. With the shifting of PAFs to the new sites, the government/ THDC initiated a number of developmental activities, like construction of roads, drinking-water facilities, and temples from which the original habitats are also equally benefited. Most of the time, resettlers negotiated with old habitants before shifting. Table 6.14 shows that about 84% of resettlers in urban areas and 78% of resettlers in rural areas have negotiated with old inhabitants. This type of pre-consultation with old inhabitants facilitated smooth shifting process and cooperation from old inhabitants wherever necessary. The PAFs reported that most of the time (89% in urban areas and 98% in rural areas) they got positive response from the old inhabitants and neighbours in getting help in their settlement (table 6.15). Many of the PAFs reported that (98% of urban and 96% of rural PAFs) the local inhabitants in resettlement areas have become friends within a short period of time (graph 6.8). Most of the time, the PAFs have not faced any disputes with old inhabitants. 76% of urban resettlers and 94% of rural resettlers did not faced any disputes with old habitants (table 6.17).

Graph 6.7 Whether the Households Have Any Disputes with Other Persons

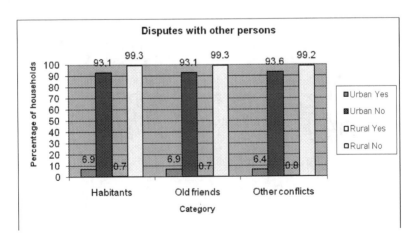

Table 6.14 Whether the Household Negotiated with Old Habitants before Shifting

	Urban	Rural	Total
Yes	83.8	78.3	80.5
No	16.2	21.7	19.5
Total	100.0 (150)	100.0 (200)	100.0 (350)

Table 6.15 Attitude of the Habitants in the New Area

	Urban	Rural	Total
Yes	89.4	97.6	93.9
No	10.6	2.4	6.11
Total	100.0 (150)	100.0 (200)	100.0 (350)

Graph 6.8 Whether the New Habitants are friendly

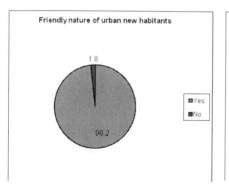
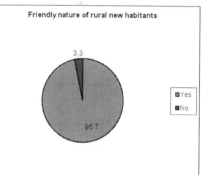

Table 6.17 Whether the Household Face Any Disputes with Old Habitants

	Urban	Rural	Total
Yes	24.4	6.2	14.4
No	75.6	93.8	85.6
Total	100.0 (150)	100.0 (200)	100.0 (350)

About the timeliness of handing over properties and compensation by the THDC/state government after completion of necessary legal formalities, 93% of urban households responded positively, while 84% of households responded positively in rural resettlement sites (table 6.18). However, about 25% of urban households and about 80% of rural households did not hand over their assets to THDC (table 6.19). This led to delays in the transfer of the new assets legally on the resettler's name. About 68% of households got legally transferred assets in urban settlements, while only about 57% of rural resettlers got legally transferred assets (table 6.20).

Table 6.18 Whether after Completion of Necessary Legal Formalities the Corporation Has Possessed the Resettler's Old Assets

	Urban	Rural	Total
Yes	93.3	84.0	87.5
No	6.7	16.0	12.5
Total	100.0 (150)	100.0 (200)	100.0 (350)

Table 6.19 If Yes, the Household Handed Over the Assets to THDC

	Urban	Rural	Total
Yes	74.7	20.0	63.2
No	25.3	80.0	36.8
Total	100.0 (150)	100.0 (200)	100.0 (350)

Table 6.20 Whether the Corporation Has Transferred the Assets Legally on the Resettler's Family Name

	Urban	Rural	Total
Yes	68.0	44.9	57.4
No	32.0	55.1	42.6
Total	100.0 (150)	100.0 (200)	100.0 (350)

In some cases, there was a delay of up to ten years, especially in rural resettlements, in transferring the assets to PAFs name (the resettler's) from the THDC due to many formalities and government procedures (table 6.21). As a policy of rehabilitation, THDC offered employment in the corporation/government irrigation department. About 17% of PAFs in urban areas and about 13% of PAFs in rural resettlements reported that their family members are working either in THDC or irrigation department (table 6.22).

Table 6.21 If Yes, Time Taken for That Transfer of Assets

No. of Years	Urban	Rural
≤1	10.7	7.5
2	5.3	6
3	4.0	2
4	4.7	1.5
5	2.7	4
6	1.3	0.5
7	3.3	0
8	2.7	0.5
9	0.0	0
≥10	2.0	6.5

The aspect of the rehabilitation was that the rehabilitation policy was uniform among all the oustees, irrespective of their skills, occupation, etc. Hence, many of the PAFs were of the opinion that the assistance provided was not based on the skills and the needs of the households (table 6.23).

Table 6.22 Whether Any of the Family Members Is Working in UP Irrigation Department or THDC

	Urban	Rural	Total
Yes	17.1	13.0	14.7
No	82.9	87.0	85.3
Total	100.0	100.0	100.0
	(150)	(200)	(350)

Table 6.23 Whether the Assistance Provided Is Based on the Skills and Needs of the Household

	Urban	Rural	Total
Yes	41.8	41.6	41.7
No	58.2	58.4	58.3
Total	100.0	100.0	100.0
	(150)	(200)	(350)

Table 6.24 If No, Needs of the Household

	Urban	Rural
Employment	46.7	28.0
Suitable land	46.7	0.0
More compensation	0.0	22.5

Only 42% of the PAFs were of the opinion that the assistance provided was based on the skills and needs of the households, and the remaining 58% of PAFs thought otherwise. Most of the urban PAFs were of the opinion that more emphasis would have been given in creating employment opportunities and providing suitable land which can be cultivatable (table 6.24). Rural PAFs were of the opinion that providing employment and providing more compensation for land and buildings should have been the highest priority. Majority of the PAFs (69%) were of the opinion that they were consulted before the rehabilitation by the authorities in urban areas, while only 63% of the PAFs in rural areas were consulted before rehabilitation (graph 6.9). Majority of the PAFs (92% among urban areas and 89% among rural areas) were of the opinion that information regarding the submerged area has been received by the households earlier.

Graph 6.9 Whether before Replacement the Consultation Has Been Taken Place by the Authorities

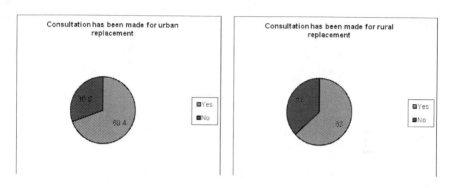

The PAFs were expecting huge rehabilitation packages. This has been revealed by ASCI socio-economic study conducted in 1993. Though the R & R package was attractive, PAFs consider the package offered by THDC was low (table 6.26). The main reasons for dissatisfaction were less compensation and less attractive business and market conditions in urban areas. In rural areas, most of the PAFs are dissatisfied with less compensation, lack of employment opportunities, and lack of suitability of land for agricultural purposes (table 6.27). Most of the PAFs (about 50%) also expressed their unwillingness to shift to new resettlement areas (table 6.28) due to lack of employment and business opportunities in new settlements and lack of supporting services and amenities (table 6.29). However, about 65% of resettlers both in rural and urban areas expressed that grievance redressal machinery is helpful in solving the problems in replacement (graph 6.10).

Panoramic view of Raiwala.

Table 6.26 Whether the Household Are Satisfied with the Assistance Given by THDC

	Urban	Rural	Total
Yes	29.1	32.5	31.2
No	70.9	67.5	68.8
Total	100.0	100.0	100.0
	(150)	(200)	(350)

Table 6.27 If No, What Are the Reasons

	Urban	Rural
Business not good	7.3	0.0
Less compensation	26.7	42.5
Market not good	9.3	0.0
Transport not good	2.7	2.0
No employment	4.7	7.5
Facilities not good	4.7	2.0
Bad bureaucratic behaviour	0.0	2.0
Education facilities	0.0	2.0
Medical facilities	0.0	2.0
Not suitable land	0.0	5.5

Table 6.28 Households' Preparedness to Shift to the New Place

	Urban	Rural	Total
Yes	49.5	52.1	51.2
No	50.5	47.9	48.8
Total	100.0 (150)	100.0 (200)	100.0 (350)

Table 6.29 If No, What Are the Reasons

	Urban	Rural
Employment	25.5	7.8
Business	25.5	0.0
Other amenities	49.0	25.6
Less compensation	0.0	42.2
Land is not suitable	0.0	24.4
Total	100.0 (150)	100.0 (200)

Graph 6.10 Whether the Grievances Redressal Machinery Is Helpful in Solving the Problem and Replacement

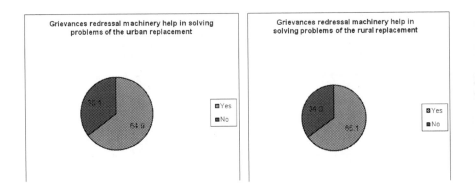

The other civic amenities like safe drinking water, sanitation, and the infrastructure developed by the THDC created a healthier atmosphere in the rehabilitated sites compared to the areas where they have stayed earlier, leading to the improvement in the living conditions of the PAPs.

From Food Insecurity to Adequate Nutrition

Expenses on food increased in absolute term. Diversified consumption pattern evolved, and fruits, vegetables, milk, and ready-to-cook foods have increased their share in the food basket both in rural and urban areas (table 5.11 and table 5.13). Increase in the expenses on food is significantly higher in case of rural households compared to urban households.

Commercial crop (sugar cane) cultivation in Banjarawala.

Park in Dehrakhas.

School

School in Dehrakhas.

Government hospital in Dehrakhas.

Dormitory in Raiwala.

Chapter 7

Summary and Conclusions

Construction of large storage dams involves large-scale submergence of land, often resulting in displacement of people. Implementation of R & R involves acquisition of land in submergence area as well as in resettlement colonies, besides creation of other civic, public, and infrastructure facilities. Acquisition of land for public purpose displaces people, forcing them to give up their homes, assets, and means of livelihood. Apart from depriving them of their lands, livelihood, and resource base, displacement has other traumatic psychological and sociocultural consequences.

The completion of multipurpose Tehri dam project was a landmark achievement in the history of river valley projects in India. The rehabilitation and resettlement works carried out in Tehri project have been on a massive scale.

Analytical Framework

The first socio-economic study carried out by the ASCI in 1993 was a benchmark survey to evaluate the project and its impact and also to build a socio-economic profile of the households to understand the conditions before and after R & R. The survey also documented the perceptions, views, and suggestions of the rehabilitated households. The present study is an updated

120

version of the previous study, and it compares with the results of the first survey to understand any changes.

The field survey has been designed based on impoverishment risks and reconstruction (IRR) model, which assesses the intrinsic risks that cause impoverishment through displacement, as well as the effectiveness of the rehabilitation policy to counteract—eliminate or mitigate—these risks through rehabilitation and resettlement. It is believed that this impoverishment risks and reconstruction (IRR) model substantively adds to the tools of explaining, diagnosing, assessing, predicting, and planning of the effectiveness of R & R policies implementation.

The sample of the households was drawn using two-stage sampling procedure. In the first stage, the villages were selected, and at the second stage, the households were selected. A total of 350 sample households were surveyed, where 200 were rural and 150 were urban households, along with 20 institutional respondents in New Tehri Town. Detailed data were collected from the affected households on socio-economic aspects both before and after rehabilitation. This can give an overall idea about how the socio-economic conditions of the households have changed because of their displacement. Data on the satisfactory levels on the civic facilities provided by the THDC in those rehabilitated colonies were also collected and compared with the amenities they had earlier in their villages.

Social Background

Social background of the sample households indicates that most of them are Hindus, which include all sections of the community, like upper castes and backward castes and weaker sections. The distance between previous and current location of the urban PAPs is less when compared with rural PAPs.

The age profile of rural and urban households is almost similar for all age groups. Majority of the population are in the prime-age group, which indicates that most of them are relatively young and capable of making adjustments with the current location.

The average family size is about 5.4 for both urban and rural sample households. The overall sex ratio is around 862, which indicates unfavourable gender situation among households for women, particularly in rural households.

Educational Level

The level of education of persons increased marginally among all PAPs after rehabilitation because most of the resettlement sites are situated in suburban/urban areas, and also THDC/GoUK has taken initiatives in establishing schools within reach for all households. The quality of education in terms of infrastructure (like building and playground) and other facilities like sanitation, drinking water, ventilation, furniture, etc. have improved a lot in the newly constructed rehabilitated colonies. The accessibility of the school from their houses is also made easy with the road network developed by the THDC, which was absent in the previous locations.

Accessibility to Land

The number of landowners having land up to 2 acres increased significantly after rehabilitation, and the current market price of their land is significantly higher when compared with the old land. The average size of land holding of the sample households increased from 1.7 acres before displacement to 1.9 acres after displacement.

Irrigation facilities have been increased significantly after rehabilitation. The THDC has developed/constructed irrigation canals/channels to most of the agricultural lands provided to the PAPs where such type of system was not present in the previous location. As a result, now farmers are cultivating three crops in a year. The cropping pattern also changed to more remunerative crops, like paddy, sugar cane, wheat, and potato. Most the farmers in suburban areas who got only 0.5 acre are cultivating vegetable crops and selling it in nearby market even though most of the PAPs are dissatisfied with the underutilization of the allotted 0.5-acre land for any commercial/non-farm activities due to lack of markets, training, and awareness.

Employment

Employment and income levels have been increased significantly. Opportunities for rural PAPs have been increased because they have allotted agricultural land with irrigation facility which helps in cultivating short-duration, high-yielding varieties of crops and they have started cultivating commercial crops by using modern farming techniques and equipments. The PAPs rehabilitated close to urban areas are benefited by the constructed shops, cultivating vegetables, fruits, flowers, etc. in their allotted land. In addition to that, they had a chance to get work in industries, service, transport, and other sectors which are available in cities only. THDC has given jobs to workmen and supervisors and ordered the contractors of the THDC to recruit unskilled workers, clerical staff, and supervisors. THDC awarded small-sized contracts for some of the PAPs and gave special preference in local developmental works. The state government also initiated various self-employment/income-generating schemes for the PAPs.

Livestock has reduced after rehabilitation, which results in income from dairy and goat-rearing being reduced significantly; however, income from other trade and construction-related activities, like electrical work and plumbing, has been increased. Most of the households do not own any farm implements before and after rehabilitation.

Housing

The THDC has given a one-room flat to the economically weaker landless oustees at free of cost in the rehabilitated area. Houses of most of the PAPs in the rural and urban areas were constructed in a modern way with sophisticated furnishings. The number of households staying in the cement/pucca houses increased significantly after rehabilitation. The household appliances, like radio, TV, and vehicles, have increased a lot after rehabilitation.

PAFs got compensated for land, house, shops, trees, and assets based on market rates prevailing at the time of rehabilitation. Apart from this, they have received various allowances/incentives for shifting, for construction of house, for decoration of house, for food, for fertilizer and seeds, etc.

Other Basic Needs

Expenditure on food has increased significantly. Diversified consumption pattern evolved, and fruits, vegetables, milk, and ready-to-cook foods have increased their share in food basket both in rural and urban areas.

The THDC gave much importance to the healthcare by constructing hospitals, primary healthcare centres, and dispensaries wherever necessary. The road network of the rehabilitated colonies also helped the patients reach the healthcare centres in time, leading to the decrease of mortality and morbidity rates. The share of income spent on health increased significantly in overall expenditure across all income groups both in urban and rural PAPs.

The other civic amenities like safe drinking water, sanitation, and community infrastructures developed by the THDC created a healthier atmosphere in the rehabilitated sites compared to the areas where they have stayed earlier, leading to the improvement in the living conditions of the PAPs.

Expenditure on Superior Goods

The expenditure incurred on vehicles, transport, and entertainment has increased significantly in both the urban and rural PAPs. These expenditure categories are at the higher hierarchy of human needs, which indicates that most the PAPs are at higher hierarchy of human needs and socio-economic development.

Majority of the sample households were satisfied with the uninterrupted power supply, and the number of hours of power supply has been increased tremendously after the rehabilitation.

Social Inclusion

Most of the PAFs reported that they have no disputes with the local population. Most of the time, the host population helped the resettlers in establishing themselves in the new place.

Women Development

Most of the rural and urban respondents expressed that there is no discrimination, no violence, and no restrictions against women, and they are participating actively in social and economic life at their newly developed rehabilitated locations. The socio-economic profile of the women after displacement in terms of status in the village and at home has been increased significantly. Source of income and employment of women in traditional activities has been decreased marginally, but other employment opportunities and educational facilities for women increased significantly as they moved to suburban and urban areas when compared to their previous locations, which are mostly remote and lack any employment opportunities for women.

Recommendations

> The PAPs, especially educated youth and women, should be provided training on entrepreneurship and other development activities in the areas like dairy, poultry, goat-rearing, beekeeping, sericulture, aquaculture, mushroom cultivation, food processing, establishment of nurseries, seed storage, fodder cultivation, vermiculture, medicinal plants, and cottage industries, leading to employment generation and sustainable economic development of the region.

> Rural artisans and rural industries in handloom, handicrafts, and khadi and village industries should be strengthened by providing training on technology upgradation and modernization.

> Training and counselling should be provided for maximum utilization of the existing available local resources with minimum expenditure.

> Local engineering college, university, and Krishi Vigyan Kendras should be nominated as nodal agencies for entrepreneurship, education, and agriculture respectively to meet the above educational/training needs.

> The PAPs should be sensitized on various government schemes for maximum utilization of ongoing government schemes by PAPs. Awareness camps should be set up with the active participation of local NGOs on government programmes on mother-and-child health, adult education, and sanitation.

> The youth of New Tehri Town can be trained as tourist guides because the dam has more potential to grow as a tourist place.

> The New Tehri Town has more potential to grow as tourist place, so the THDC can establish linkages with various tourism development corporations and agencies to develop tourism in the area. This can lead to the creation of more employment in sectors like business, transport, and other services for youth of the NTT.

- ➤ The common properties like parks, dormitories, shopping complex, etc. are unutilized/underutilized. They were developed/constructed by the THDC, but the THDC or PAPs are not maintaining them properly because of low density of population. It would be better if they form a committee with the rehabilitated PAPs and maintain the common properties and allow the people residing in nearby areas to utilize the properties on commercial/fee basis. The income earned from this can be used for the development and maintenance of these facilities.
- ➤ Some of the urban and rural PAPs are facing the problem with safe drinking water. It is ideal if the THDC can do alternative arrangements like digging tube wells and constructing overhead water tanks with pipelines wherever necessary to overcome the problem.
- ➤ The recreation facilities, like movie theatres and amusement parks, at the rehabilitated colonies should be developed.
- ➤ The entrepreneurs should be encouraged to start vocational training institutions, like ITIs, polytechnic colleges, and agricultural colleges, in the new colonies.
- ➤ The existing grievance redressal mechanism that is functioning needs to be further strengthened by including independent experts for periodical review.
- ➤ Cut-off areas need to be given special emphasis on priority basis to link up with mainland.

References

Somayaji, S., & Talwar, S. (Eds.). (2011). *Development–induced Displacement, Rehabilitation and Resettlement in India: Current Issues and Challenges.* Taylor & Francis.

Dreze, Jean and Sen, Amartya(1996) India Economic Development and Social Opportunity, OUP, New Delhi, 1996.

Scudder, Thayer(1997): Social Impacts of Large Dams in Large Dams; Learning from the Past, Looking at the Future, IUCN/WB, Gland, 1997.

McCully, Patrick(1996): Silenced Rivers, the Ecology and Politics of Large Dams, Zed Books, London and New Jersey, 1996.

China Report(1999):: Jing, Jun: Displacement, Resettlement, Rehabilitation, Reparation and Development -China Report, July 1999.

Printed in the United States
By Bookmasters